To Bill & Heather,

I hope you enjoy the book!

Love & blessings,

Cosandra

p.s. When are we having that Trivial Pursuit rematch?!?

ALSO BY CASANDRA HART

"The Sovereign Soul—A Story of Personal Power"

ADVENTURES OF A MYSTIC MEDIUM

Amazing True Psychic Stories – Tips & Truisms

CASANDRA HART

BALBOA
PRESS
A DIVISION OF HAY HOUSE

Copyright © 2014 Casandra Hart.

All rights reserved. No part of this book may be used or reproduced by any means, graphic, electronic, or mechanical, including photocopying, recording, taping or by any information storage retrieval system without the written permission of the publisher except in the case of brief quotations embodied in critical articles and reviews.

Balboa Press books may be ordered through booksellers or by contacting:

Balboa Press
A Division of Hay House
1663 Liberty Drive
Bloomington, IN 47403
www.balboapress.com
1 (877) 407-4847

Because of the dynamic nature of the Internet, any web addresses or links contained in this book may have changed since publication and may no longer be valid. The views expressed in this work are solely those of the author and do not necessarily reflect the views of the publisher, and the publisher hereby disclaims any responsibility for them.

The author of this book does not dispense medical advice or prescribe the use of any technique as a form of treatment for physical, emotional, or medical problems without the advice of a physician, either directly or indirectly. The intent of the author is only to offer information of a general nature to help you in your quest for emotional and spiritual well-being. In the event you use any of the information in this book for yourself, which is your constitutional right, the author and the publisher assume no responsibility for your actions.

Any people depicted in stock imagery provided by Thinkstock are models, and such images are being used for illustrative purposes only.
Certain stock imagery © Thinkstock.

Printed in the United States of America.

ISBN: 978-1-4525-9447-7 (sc)
ISBN: 978-1-4525-9448-4 (hc)
ISBN: 978-1-4525-9449-1 (e)

Library of Congress Control Number: 2014904950

Balboa Press rev. date: 04/09/2014

ARE YOU PSYCHIC?

Take the quiz inside to reveal your personal 'GPS'

or

'Great Physic Score'!

For my mother through whom came my life,
my name and my gift of prophecy!

ACKNOWLEDGEMENT

My ego would like to have you believe it wrote this book all by itself! I thanked it for sharing, and will now attempt to give thanks where thanks are due. Let me begin by acknowledging the many enlightened authors whose books on spirituality I have devoured over the last forty years. Many of these same authors now publish under the Hay House banner which leads me to my next acknowledgement. The small blue book, "Heal Your Body", by Louise Hay was one of my earliest introductions to the power within each of us. Thank you.

To my friend and mentor, Tom, my sincere thank you for insisting I channel every day and also in public in order to hone my skills. During such a reading my wonderful group of guides, who call themselves, "The Council of One", first made themselves known. They then went on to write my first book, "The Sovereign Soul – A Story of Personal Power" through me and continue to assist in all my psychic readings and writing. I thank them in advance for all the adventures still awaiting manifestation and I thank you dear reader for picking up this book!

MY MANTRA
"Don't do anything that isn't fun!
Happiness is a decision!"

MY MISSION
"To Educate & Inspire."

MY SECRET TO HAPPINESS
"Want what shows up! After all, you ordered it!
If you can't change the circumstance,
change how you feel about it!
Don't bitch—fix!"

MY DISCLAIMER:

These are my stories as I have experienced them. They are my truth. Names and places have been changed to respect individuals' privacy where requested; however, they happened as written. As a medium I communicate often with those who have 'crossed over' and consequently, I may have a different perspective on death and dying than my readers. It is not my intent to minimize the pain of separation when a loved one dies, but to give hope that they live on and even communicate with us, thus my light hearted approach. My hope is that you read with enjoyment and allow your mind to entertain the existence of more than the five senses perceive. I reserve the right, as all can, to change my perceptions as new life lessons come my way. However, if you stumble upon some Truth in these pages, you are welcome to take it as yours!

Love & blessings to all of you,
Casandra

ADVENTURES OF A MYSTIC MEDIUM
Amazing True Psychic Stories, Tips & Truisms

CONTENTS

1. Destiny or Self-Fulfilling Prophesy?............1
2. Death at the Door..............6
3. A California Rose..............10
4. Who Are Our Babies?..............15
5. I'm Forgetting..............18
6. The Kiss..............22
7. It's A Gusher!..............25
8. The Woodstove..............28
9. The Goodbye..............31
10. Fate and Forgiveness..............36
11. The Funeral Flower..............42
12. A Guardian Angel?..............46
13. What's In a Name?..............50
14. "Another Story"–The Winter Funeral..............54
15. Damian and the Purple Pants..............58
16. The Three Friends..............62
17. The Face of Evil..............65
18. Todd and the Tower..............69
19. The Coma Connection..............74
20. Snakes in the Streets!..............78
21. Dennis and the Dog..............82
22. The Daisies..............88
23. An Old Story..............91
24. The Big Sadness..............95
25. A Mover and a Shaker!..............99
26. Stabbed in the Back!..............104
27. A 'Rock' From The 'Rock'!..............110
28. Fred in the Closet..............114
29. Is It A Little Boy?..............117

30.	The Dragonfly Day	121
31.	The Christmas Bell	125
32.	A Burned Out Basement of a Heart	129
33.	Doubting Thomas	135
34.	Lovers and Friends	140
35.	Your Future is in Your Hands!	146
36.	Death at My Door Again?	150
37.	Breakfast in New England	155
38.	The Father on the Stairs	161
39.	A Multiple Egg Producer!	164
40.	The Killing Place	168
41.	The Promise	178
42.	The Boy on the Stairs	182
43.	Six Thousand and Forty Six Little Blue Balls	186
44.	The Birthday Gift	190
45.	The Wrong Way Out	194
46.	Let Me Entertain You!	198
47.	Welcome Home!	203

TERMS THAT MAY HELP

As defined in 'Webster's New world Dictionary' OR used in the context of this book.

Acknowledge	to say that you accept or do not deny the truth or existence of (something)
Addiction	Attachment, even when known to be harmful, to a substance, behavior, person – anything external to the self - which prevents intimacy with the self.
Archetype	pattern of behaviour or prototype, pure form which embodies the fundamental character of a thing
Channel	any means of passage (as in passage of information from one reality to another)
Codependent	dependent on the needs of or control of another. Placing a lower priority on one's own needs, while being excessively preoccupied with the needs of others; that is, "to love until it hurts"! [1]
Council	a group of people called together for discussion or advice
Denial	a refusal to acknowledge; disclaimer of connection with, as, the denial of a fault charged on one
G.P.S.	Great Psychic Score; Great Psychic Source; Great Personal Source; Guided Personal Script;
'Home'	alignment with the divine self
Medium	one through whom messages are supposedly sent from the dead
Metaphysics	a branch of philosophy that seeks to explain the nature of being and reality; that is, 'more' than the physical

Mystic	a believer in mysticism (really?)
Mysticism	any doctrine that asserts knowledge of spiritual truths
Psychic	beyond known physical processes; one apparently sensitive to forces beyond the physical world
Self-Actualize	to have achieved the full realization of one's potential and true self.[9]
Sovereign	independent of all others
TRUISM:	A tested belief that led me to peace. If it is not ascribed to any other mind, it came through mine.
TIPS:	Thoughts and actions I've designed to produce openness to personal peace.

Truism: Knowing what is happening around you is not nearly as important as what you think about what is happening around you. Casandra

AMAZING ADVENTURE #1
DESTINY OR SELF-FULFILLING PROPHESY?

1963.
This is a true story.

I was fifteen. He was twenty one. He came into my life as the direct result of a promise I would not break.

It was the summer of 1963 and our family had just returned from its annual vacation. My father, a working man, had piled the tiny imported car high with a wife, four children, luggage and the family dog and taken all of us camping for two weeks. It was the only type of holiday which fit our budget.

We didn't care. We thought it was wonderful! I particularly found it just grand for I had fallen in love for the first time!

He was tall, blonde and handsome! Every girl in the camp was after him and because I had little faith in myself, I walked the dog and avoided the throngs of girls surrounding him.

To some it may have appeared I was playing hard to get, but I was not at that level of sophistication. It was with absolute disbelief that I stood mute when he introduced himself and asked if he could walk with me!

Two weeks flew by and I'm sure my feet never quite touched the ground! Attentive and kind, never once did he do more than hold my hand and place a few sweet kisses on my lips. I was in love!

It was agony to leave. He had asked for my address and said he would write. He never did, but for years, I would still see his golden face and sweet smile as he had waved his goodbye.

"But you promised!! The words of my best friend jolted me back to reality. My family had been home for a day now and I had taken up residence at the mailbox awaiting letters that would never come.

"I don't want to go," I said flatly.

"How can you be so mean? You promised you would go camping with my brothers and me!" she wailed.

"Now I'll be stuck with just them and my dad! You have to come! You promised!"

And indeed I had, just a few days before my family had left on our vacation. It had seemed like a great idea to go camping again with my best friend as soon as my family and I returned. Why not? It was summer and they were going to a different park and besides, her twin brother was really cute! How was I to know I would no longer want to do anything else but wait for the mailman??

My camping gear was loaded in her family car. I waved goodbye to my folks and the mailbox and headed off to the campgrounds!

Looking back, I often think my best friend's father should have been given a parenting medal. A single father when such was unheard of, he raised five children from the ages of eighteen through eight all on his own. My friend was seventeen and a handful!! Far more sophisticated than I, she was a boy magnet and I adored her! Her father never had a chance. Always two steps ahead of him, she was on the prowl for boys! It was all she thought about. Consequently, we walked miles scouting out every campsite, and when she discovered one with two single guys, we walked more miles, it seemed, back and forth in front of it!

Not surprisingly, they approached us as we appeared to be sitting casually on the beach.

Unimpressed, I gave them an aloof once over. The short one, I thought, was kind of cute, but that tall, skinny one was certainly not my type. Besides, my heart was already taken!

They chatted us up and introduced themselves. The short one was Italian with swarthy brown skin, flashing white toothed smile, stocky build and affable style. The tall one was German, darkly tanned, with jet black hair, and only a rare smile or word leaving a taciturn face. They couldn't have been more different.

"You girls want to go for a hike?" the short one asked.

The tall one shot him a pained look. He doesn't like me either I thought, but before I could say no, my friend had answered, "Sure!"

I gave her a dirty look but also to no avail. She had already staked her claim. I could see she liked the short one.

What are friends for, right? I knew she wanted to go so of course I had to tag along.

Grumpily, I got in line. The end of the line it soon appeared for the tall, skinny one immediately took the lead with disgruntled me bringing up the rear.

About twenty minutes into the hike, something very strange happened. As I watched the quiet, tall one take charge, moving effortlessly, breaking trail and leading the way up a steep cliff face, admiration began to grow. Here was a leader. Perhaps, I had overlooked something special.

It was the rebound effect as well. I was a vulnerable fifteen year old girl from the country, unsophisticated in the ways of the heart. He was a city boy, employed, and supremely sure of himself. He had not been interested in what was commonly referred to as ' jail bait' but in spite of himself, kept spending time as part of what my friend's father had dubbed, ' the fearsome foursome'!

And so it was that several weeks after the camping trip, he appeared at my door for an official date.

My mother stood behind me as I greeted a very formally dressed, tall, serious young man and as he made his way to sit in our living room, she took me by the hand and whispered into my ear, "That's the man you're going to marry!"

"Don't be ridiculous," I whispered back… "I don't even like him!"

"You'll see," she said with a knowing smile and nod that gave me chills.

Her statement was striking because my maternal grandmother had been psychic. Her ability to see departed souls was family legend and my mother, it appeared, had inherited the gift of prophecy. On several occasions, she had accurately predicted someone's death because she was unable to see their aura. This ability had understandably frightened her so she had had no desire to develop it further.

Even though I shrugged off her words at the time, I must admit, they influenced me. Perhaps it was the reason we dated for a few months even though I really didn't care for him. Eventually, I found the courage to break it off. It was not easy for very few people ever said no to him. I lied, saying my parents had forbidden me to see him because he was so much older.

"My mother's prediction must have been wrong," I mused as I watched him angrily back out of our driveway.

Months passed. I went on to fall in love again. He was another beautiful blonde boy, so much like my first crush, and so unlike the tall, skinny one. We dated throughout my senior year in high school and my hiker was forgotten.

Then one day the phone rang. It was three years later and I was once again on the rebound. I was older, but wiser?

He would be in town taking a course. Would I see him, the familiar voice on the line asked?

Was it destiny or belief in destiny?

Who knows?

I said yes.

My mother's prediction came to pass. Two years later the adventurous hiker and I were married, but that is another story!

TRUISM: "The retreat to death is not the end of conflict." Course in Miracles

AMAZING ADVENTURE #2

DEATH AT THE DOOR

1970.
This is a true story.

To say that my family beliefs were threaded through with French Canadian folk lore would have been accurate. My mother's and grandmother's superstitions and physic abilities were well worn tales told around the kitchen table while copious amounts of black tea were consumed. We loved the stories that made the hair on the back of our neck stand up and filled us with questions. Was all that our five senses told us true regarding our present twentieth century experience, we wondered?

Thus it was, on this particular morning, as a young bride and mother, in my bed half asleep and half awake, listening for the stirrings of my new baby daughter, I was startled awake by three very loud, distinct knocks on the front door and knew enough to ask, "Who is it for?"

You see, one of the oft told stories of my family was that death, 'came knocking at the door' and if we asked who it was to claim, we would be given the answer.

Silently, in my mind I whispered the ominous question and received the name of an uncle on my father's side. At this point he appeared to be in reasonably good health, albeit a heavy drinker now for many years, but of robust personality and often described as someone, 'you couldn't kill with an axe'!

I don't exactly know how I 'knew' but I sensed his death would be within the next six months or so. I mentioned this fact to my husband and because this particular uncle was not close to us, nor had we heard he was ill, I murmured something to the effect that I was probably wrong and went about my day.

He died of cancer six months later. The disease had progressed rapidly and had been kept secret from the family until shortly before his death.

I have since experienced this phenomenon on four other occasions.

The next was a year or so later, when once again awakened by three loud, sharp raps on what sounded like our front door, I rolled over in bed and asked somewhat fearfully, "Who is it for?"

Again an answer came. This time it was a dear friend of my parents. He was not yet sixty, appeared to be in good health, although they had not spoken to him for some months as they had moved away and now saw him less frequently. The revelation caused me some sadness for he had been very much around as I had been growing up and I was fond of him.

I was not then surprised when several months later I received a telephone call from my mother telling me that he had been diagnosed with lung cancer and was not expected to live much longer. Within the year death had claimed him.

Two years later another set of three early morning knocks and another name foretold the death of an older man whom I had been very fond of as a teenager and who cancer also claimed in his sixth decade of life.

There seemed to be neither rhyme nor reason to these precognitions. There was nothing to be done to change the outcome and the timing was very erratic, ranging from a few months to several years. It was almost as if once a soul had decided to depart this life reverberations went out into the cosmos summoning the beginning of the end! Death on its way, meandering at times, arriving rapidly at others, but nevertheless, its approach foretold.

Twice more I have heard death's knock-both occasions for sisters of my dear mother. An older brother and she are all who are left of a large family of twelve children. I don't know if I will 'know' when her time is at hand.

In my sixty fifth year now as I write this story, I am very grateful I have not heard my own name spoken in answer to the question, "Who is it for?"

That day will surely come. Will I respond to that familiar knock as that of a friend come to take me home? That just may be another story for another to write!

TRUISM: "Suicide is the biggest problem in the world that the world is in total denial of. It's the dirty little secret of the ego. More people die from suicide than are killed by all of the wars and all of the crime in the world combined." Gary Renard

AMAZING ADVENTURE #3

A CALIFORNIA ROSE

1973.
This is a true story.

It was late. We were tired from the drive. Sunday dinner at my parents' home some thirty miles away had become a tradition since our marriage several years before. A young bride and new mother, I hadn't yet mastered the art of the perfect roast beef dinner, so I assume my husband thought my mother's worth the drive.

Our daughter, now a sleepy three and a half year old bundle, sighed contentedly as I lowered her into her bed. Too frugal to hire babysitters, we took her everywhere with us and she had learned to adapt to sleeping wherever she found herself.

It was the end of April. I remember because we had been celebrating my father's birthday and also because I was concerned that I had not yet uncovered my rose bushes from their winter sleep. Moving into our new home, I had inherited a beautiful rose garden, but had had absolutely no concept of how to care for it. That's were my husband's sister had come in. We had met when her brother and I were dating. Quiet and eight years older than I, she nevertheless always made time for me and I could see that she was a gentle and kind person. Shortly after we met though, she and her new husband and baby daughter moved to California to live.

I had always dreamed of visiting California. Isn't there a song by that title? Before our marriage when I was just nineteen, having completed my first year of grade school teaching, I had jumped at his offer to accompany him on a visit to his sister's home! I was going to live my dream – California here I come!

Because we were not married, his mother drove with us as our chaperone. It seems quaint now, but that was how it was then. Nice girls just didn't!

Three long days on the road made us very happy to arrive at the lovely Spanish style home in San Mateo. His sister was a wonderful hostess. Unfortunately her husband was not. His arrogant behaviour bordered on abusive to his wife and he lost little time informing me, a total stranger, that the only reason he had married her was because she had been pregnant!

Needless to say, as our stay went on, my heart went out to the young wife and mother who did everything she could to make her husband and guests happy. The harder she tried, the worse he became it seemed, leaving her to retreat into her beautiful gardens. She had cultivated a small Eden in their back yard, fruit trees bursting with succulent ripe apricots and plums, flowering vines, a riot of blooming perennials and annuals and her proudest accomplishment, her roses! It was very difficult to grow them in the California climate - the bug population seemed to love them as much as she did!

As we walked through her gardens, she talked about the plants, teaching me a great deal. She rarely mentioned her situation for she was a proud person and determined to make her marriage work. In fact they were planning a second child she told me. By this time, I thoroughly disliked her husband's controlling, abusive ways. I had never seen a man treat his wife that way. Perhaps, I should have heeded her warning when one day she asked me pointedly, "Do you love my brother?'

Before I could answer, she went on, "He's not for you. Don't rush into anything."

She didn't need to worry, I thought to myself. I was not about to get married! Just finding my own power, my life seemed spread out before me like a great adventure. How then did I happen to walk down the aisle only two years later? Well, that is another story!

She had flown in to be in our wedding party. Things were not going well in California, it seemed. Whispered discussions with her parents would stop abruptly when I entered the room. Her mother, busy packing family heirlooms to send back with her, admonished her daughter to, 'make a good home for your husband.' I gathered divorce was not an option in this family! Better to suffer in silence!

A second child was born – a son. They invited us for another visit. Married and pregnant now with our first child, it was my first flight ever and I was just thrilled to be going anywhere! The visit was tense. His sister's unhappiness was palpable. Even in the warmest of weather, she wore long sleeves. While we were in the garden one day, I was shocked to see an ugly scar on her wrist. As I stared open mouthed, she tried to be casual saying, "Oh yes, I fell when I was carrying a glass milk jug."

It seemed implausible to me, but I was a guest in her home – a house where women's words were not valued. Suffer in silence could have been embroidered on a sampler and hung in a place of honour! In fact it would not have been out of place in a lot of homes in the 1970's!

Shutting herself away with her new baby, rarely speaking to anyone, she did just that - suffer. The house was filled with tension. Our husbands decided upon a camping trip to the mountains, perhaps just to get away. With a screaming match over who was in charge, the trip ended disastrously.

Safely back home, married life went on. Our daughter was born, occasional letters and cards arrived from California until one day my husband informed me in a flat, dull voice that his sister had moved out into her own apartment. There was to be no discussion about it. It was the way of his family – silences and secrets.

So it was that every time I tended my roses, my thoughts would drift to the one who spent time teaching me about their care. I had gone late to bed on this April evening, dreading the six a.m. alarm which would begin my workday routine with a sleepy child awakened for transport to day care, and I resolved to spend time in the garden the next weekend. With that last thought, I fell into an exhausted sleep, only to be awakened by a blood curdling scream coming from my young daughter's room! As my feet hit the floor running, I realized what I was hearing. It made my hair stand on end!

What on earth…? What could it possibly mean? How could a child say such a thing?

Terrified, confused, I stood at the doorway of her room and saw my little girl sitting straight up in her bed, eyes closed, and then surprisingly, she calmly lay back down, fast asleep!

It was only on the following Saturday, kneeling, my hands deep in rose bush soil, hearing my husband's words, that my child's meaning became clear.

Sadly, slowly he had walked toward me. I knew something was terribly wrong. He stood, towering above me as I looked up to see his lips form the words, "My sister is dead."

He then turned on his heel and went into the house. I cried for both of us.

The date of her death had been my father's birthday.

Was it accidental or did she finally succeed in ending her unhappy life? Unanswered questions swirled around in our minds for years.

Perhaps you can be the judge. The words my baby daughter screamed out that April night, you ask?

It was simply, two short, simple exclamations and then silence.

"I want to live! I want to live!"

TRUISM: "Your children are not your children. They are the sons and daughters of life's longing for itself. They came through you, but are not from you. And though they are with you, they belong not to you." Kahil Gibran

AMAZING ADVENTURE #4

WHO ARE OUR BABIES?

1974.
This is a true story.

It was late afternoon and I was preparing dinner -one of my small family's favourites- beef stroganoff – and I was lost in thought about what was to come in the next month or so. As I worked at the stove I was keenly aware of the size of my pregnant belly. My due date was a month away and I was thinking a thought that had been with me since I had first learned I was expecting.

This was to be our second child. Our first had been a healthy girl and now I imagined a little boy was on his way. We had even picked out his name!

Lately, I had become very good at predicting the sex of all my friends' babies. This ability had attracted some attention and comment of late. It seemed I was increasingly right about other events as well. At this point, it was shrugged off as a neat parlour trick and no one really took my ability seriously, least of all I!

I had been sure I was carrying a boy.

Mindlessly stirring dinner, lost in a relaxed daydream, one hand resting contentedly on my belly, I 'heard' a small voice!

Gleefully it said, "I'm a girl, Mommy!"

I will never forget the giggle and pure sense of fun that came through in that little voice. There was such delight in not being what was expected, in being a surprise!

In the month of May, on a holiday weekend, my darling daughter presented herself! She was lovely – in fact – people would stop me on the street to remark on what an exquisite little girl she was! No doubt there!

Today she lives in South Africa. A beautiful woman who cares for animals and ironically would never eat meat! No beef stroganoff for her! I think she still delights in doing and being the unexpected, but that's another story!

TRUISM: "Your vision will become clear only when you look into your heart. Who looks outside, dreams. Who looks inside, awakens." Carl Jung

AMAZING ADVENTURE #5
I'M FORGETTING

1976.
This is a true story.

I was a busy stay–at–home mother of a new baby and a toddler. Life was hectic – too full of doing to think much about being - a blessing for there was much unease in our home. My marriage was less than satisfying, our finances were stretched to the limit and the relentless desire for more drove me daily deeper into black unhappiness.

My babies were my sunlight! I loved being a mom and I could forget myself in their smiles. As I held them in my arms and felt their warm bodies nestled against mine, I felt strangely at peace There is something almost 'otherworldly' about an innocent child's sleeping face.

There's that word –'otherworldly'. It seemed I had a fascination for all things psychic these days, reading every book about channeling and meditation I could find. This was not yet mainstream so there were few others with whom to discuss my interest. In fact, it was the best way to, 'clear a room' at a party! People would get that glazed over look and excuse themselves whenever I brought the subject up.

It turned out it could even make me uncomfortable.

Seated cross legged in the middle of my living room this fall day, both babies napping, I had decided to try TM. For those of you who are new to this spiritual stuff, it means Transcendental Meditation. Using a mantra repeated over and over again is designed to quiet the mind and eventually, with much practice, lead to 'the silence,' where inspiration can be received.

Unprepared for the experience and wanting simply to relax and release tension from my day, I was stunned and scared by what happened next!

With a whoosh of sound past my ears much like the hyper drive engines cutting in on a TV episode of Star Wars, I was transported into a milky white nothingness! No sound, nothing to see or feel, I was floating in a sea of timeless, silent space.

"Get me out of here!' my ego screamed through my mind.

And I did. I opened my eyes, uncrossed my legs, stood up and put the meditation book right back on the shelf where it stayed for several more years! I was just not ready for enlightenment it seemed.

No, it would take quite a few more brushes with the 'otherworld' before I was ready to give it credence.

That leads me to this story.

It is a tale told to me by another, but it still makes the hair on the back of my neck stand up to this day.

A young stay at home mother like me with a new baby and a toddler, this is what she had to say.

"One day, as I came upon the doorway to the nursery, laundry basket in hand, I stopped to see my three year old standing by the baby's crib, his face pressed close to the bars, eyes intently looking at his new brother and I heard him whisper, 'Tell me again what it's like over there. I'm forgetting."

Who are our babies anyway? But that is another story!

I'm Forgetting

TRUISM: "A hug is the perfect present. One size fits all and it's easy to exchange." Anonymous

AMAZING ADVENTURE #6

THE KISS

1976.
This is a true story.

Our family complete, our second daughter, was now two years of age and just beginning to talk. She often had to compete with her older sister now six, who was busy, this dinner time, telling us about her school day. A quiet child, she sat silently waiting her turn to say something. We were often just the three of us, as their father worked late. His ever present fear of lack drove him to put money before all else - even family. His stern German upbringing had shaped him to expect his children to respect and fear him.

An abusive childhood, terrors of war witnessed in his homeland, a cold, indifferent and absent father serving in the Nazi army, meant that when his father, an old man terrified of dying, had ferociously clung to life all through my second pregnancy, my husband could not find it in his heart to comfort him with his presence. Thus, her grandfather never laid dying eyes upon her beautiful little face, nor had the opportunity to welcome her to life. My husband, his son, had not seen the need to visit, and I fearing his wrath, had not insisted.

The kitchen in our new bungalow had just enough room for a table where our small family ate dinner each evening. The adjoining dining room was rarely used for it was in this very room, in the eerie shadows of the night, emerging alone from my baby daughter's room, I would shudder to 'see' the dim outline of a person, as if standing watch over the house.

This particular spring supper evening, her chubby little legs swinging from her booster chair, she played happily with her food, content to listen to her big sister.

I sat distractedly running through my mental list of things yet to be done that evening.

Her older sister's abrupt stop in mid sentence got my attention. Staring at her sister, her mouth hung open with a puzzled look upon her face. I followed her gaze only to see a once happy, carefree younger daughter now frozen, a look of sheer terror spreading across her face. Seconds ticked by as we watched every muscle in her tiny body stiffen. Absolutely rigid, she appeared to be expecting a blow. Our eyes wide, our mouths hanging open, we continued to watch as slowly a smile began to spread across her beautiful little face once again. She was aglow and her whole body softened.

What we had just witnessed had left us speechless, but as we watched her relax, we found our voices and in unison asked, 'What is it? Are you alright?"

Without a moment's hesitation, she looked at us each in turn, smiled and said in her two year old words, "Man kissed me, Mommy. It's alright. He gone now."

Calmly she went back to eating her dinner as we looked at each other in amazement. As far as we were concerned, there had been no 'man' visible in our kitchen that evening!

Who or what had made itself known to a tiny child who could still 'see'?

Had her grandfather come to say his goodbye?

We like to think so, and so she believes as well. That beautiful little girl is now a beautiful grown woman – one who has demonstrated her ability to 'see' those who have crossed over on several occasions, but that too is another story!

TRUISM: "If you can't believe – just be open to the possibility of testing for truth." Casandra

AMAZING ADVENTURE #7
IT'S A GUSHER!

1980's.
This is a true story.

It was a typical fall day and I was out walking with my father along the tree lined road that ran from their bed and breakfast, down into a small valley where his new neighbours were drilling a well. Finding sufficient water for a reliable supply was a challenge in this northern location and it looked as if the excavating had been going on for some time with no result. We stopped to observe the machinery at work and to chat with the men who were doing the drilling.

"Looks like a dry hole" one of them said. "We're down a long way and nothing yet. I think the owner's going to pack it in."

"That happens a lot in these parts," my father observed. "Let's head back to the house for lunch. I'm hungry!" he said to me.

"No, I want to wait," I answered.

"Wait for what?" he asked.

I had been sensing something strange. It was as if the ground was vibrating, moving, almost humming under my feet. Feeling unsteady, I wanted to reach out to hold on to something. The roar of rushing water was building in my ears.

"Wow!" I thought. "This is something big, something powerful!" I 'saw' water shooting high into the air flowing uncontrolled and unending!

"I can feel it," I said.

Dad looked at me strangely. "Feel what?"

"The ground ... it's shaking...the pressure is building ....they're going to hit a gusher! It's going to really blow and I want to see it!"

"Oh, I don't think so," he added, looking at me strangely.

My father was too polite to say what he really thought – you're crazy –the wells here are never that good – what you are suggesting has never happened in these parts!

Nice guy that he was, my dad waited around with me a little longer, but when his hunger got the best of him and nothing else had developed, he suggested we head back to the house.

Disappointed and doubting what I had 'seen and felt', I reluctantly agreed.

A half hour later, as we sat in the kitchen eating, a truck came roaring up our driveway, gravel flying as it came to a screeching halt. A door slammed, footsteps bounded up our back stairs, a few rapid raps on our door and then a man calling out, "Can I use your phone?!"

"Sure," Dad replied as he opened the kitchen door. "What's up -some kind of emergency?"

"Ya kinda, well no. Hell, the water's everywhere! Can't get it capped! At least thirty feet in the air! We hit a real gusher!"

Yes, artesian wells were very rare in 'those parts' as her father had said, but not impossible.

As she smiled to herself she thought, "I know what I know!' To see the future was not impossible either, but that is another set of stories!

TRUISM: "Know thyself." Socrates

AMAZING ADVENTURE #8

THE WOODSTOVE

1980's.
This is a true story.

The air was crisp and cold and we could see our breath as we trudged up the snow covered hill. Hot chocolate and the warmth of a wood fire waited for us as my father and I, completing our walk, headed for my parent's northern bed and breakfast.

We walked along in silence. My dad was a man of few words. Having little formal education, he was nevertheless possessed of wisdom, wit and an inquisitive mind. We shared many opinions, differing only when it came to what my family called, 'that psychic stuff'. However, lately in spite of himself, this very logical man, having witnessed some of my predictions come to pass, was beginning to believe there might just be something to it all!

I had been walking with my head down, straining forward, the steepness of the hill demanding my full exertion. Winded and walking slowly, finally at its crest, I raised my gaze. What I 'saw' ahead stunned and stopped me! It was almost dusk, yet the sky before me filled my view with orange, yellow and vermillion flames. Something big was on fire! I 'knew' it was a house and I also 'knew' it was not happening now but destined for the future!

My father paused beside me and stood waiting, wondering why I had come to a halt. Not wanting to alarm him, for I thought it might very well be his home destined to burn, I began walking again searching for the words to tell him what I had 'seen' but could not quite believe to be true!

"Dad," I began. "Would you do me a very big favour?"

"Sure. If I can," he answered.

"Would you promise me you will be very, very careful with your wood stove this winter?" I said.

He looked at me very strangely as he walked along beside me.

My father was always extremely vigilant - almost as if he himself worried about the very same occurrence.

"Of course, just as I always am," he answered, but there was a hesitation, a gravity, almost as if he also 'knew', I thought.

Nothing more was said that day about the incident and the winter passed without a crimson fire-filled sky.

It was spring when I heard the news. The house further down the road had been struck by lightening and because of the rural location, had burned to the ground before fire crews arrived. My parents had stood and watched the sky filled with flames from the crest of the very same hill where I had had my vision. Luckily, no one was hurt as the family was away in town for the day.

My father and I never discussed what had transpired between us on our walk that winter day, but I noticed he listened a little more attentively now when 'that psychic stuff' was discussed, but those are now other stories!

TRUISM: "Death is a doorway to yet another dream." Casandra

AMAZING ADVENTURE #9

THE GOODBYE

March 31st, 1991.
This is a true story.

Had I always been a Daddy's girl? Perhaps, but not in the sense that he doted on me, the oldest of his four daughters, but I knew he loved me unconditionally. During times when girls were not given higher education, for we would simply, 'get married and have babies', my father boldly affirmed, "My girls can do anything they want to do – no different than boys can!"

My bond with my father had formed early. My mother, who today is my mentor and friend, was at the time of my birth, a child expecting a child. Her first eighteen years of life had been spent as the youngest of twelve children in a dysfunctional family dominated by a charismatic alcoholic sexual abuser. She did her very best, but hugs and cuddles from her were not part of my early childhood.

I preferred to spend my time with my busy dad – often his co-pilot as he drove his taxi cab. It was the only way he could spend time with me and besides, I was a lively five year old and pretty good at collecting tips from the customers! I even got to spend some of those much needed tips on treats – my dad was a fair minded man!

My first 'driving lesson' was at the age of five, seated on his knee, steering the big, black 1952 Ford Meteor taxi cab, convinced I was truly in control of all that power under the hood! In charge, but watched over and protected too - that's how you felt with my dad. He wouldn't interfere, letting you learn for yourself, but he was always watchful, ready to intercede if needed. Those times in the taxi cab are still some of my best memories to this day.

Life got busy. I grew up, married and moved away. I taught school, raised two daughters and limped along in an unfulfilling marriage, but that is another story!

It was the last day of March. If you are familiar with the north I'm sure it brings to mind the type of morning greeting me. The bedroom was filled with grey dawn light, the air damp and chilly as I opened my eyes so I decided to dig back into the covers and delay the start of this dreary day!

Drifting back into sleep, I began what I can only call a lucid dream – I knew I was asleep, but it was different – I felt as if I were awake and stepping into another place where images were blurred against dark backgrounds, sounds muffled and distorted, movement like walking through water, all energy slowed down, thickened but imbued with an ominous importance, an expectance.

I was a young girl again standing shivering beside the big, black 1952 taxi cab. It was parked and as I moved closer to it, I could make out my father sitting behind the wheel. He was dressed for work with his peaked cap and his dark driver's uniform. As I peered in, he smiled at me and began to roll his window down. I looked into the misty grey interior of the cab and saw the outline of a passenger, shrouded in black, his face only a shadow. He never turned to look at me.

I looked back expectantly at my father.

Lovingly he said. "I've come to say goodbye."

"But I want to go with you. Please take me with you!" I pleaded as only a young child can. "Please!"

"Where I'm going you can't come," he said matter-of-factly and at that he looked over at his passenger who silently nodded. In that moment of recognition an intense pain hit my heart and I woke up shrieking, gasping for air, like a drowning swimmer fighting their way back to the surface.

"Oh my God!" I sobbed as my feet hit the floor running. "It's my father! Something has happened to my father! I have to call him! I have to warn him. He's going to die!"

As I sobbed hysterically over the bathroom sink, crouched, holding my stomach resisting the urge to wretch and searching for the phone, my husband looked at me as if I were insane.

"What now?" I'm sure he was thinking.

There had been a lot of visions coming lately as I became more involved with my own psychic development and he, feeling threatened by something he could not control nor explain, chose to dismiss it all.

"I'm sure he's fine. It's just one of your crazy dreams. It doesn't mean anything. Call him," he said, then rolled over and buried his head in the covers.

Dad had had difficult open heart surgery several years before, but had enjoyed renewed good health of late and was happier than I had seen him in a long time.

"You're probably right" I answered as I shakily dialed the phone.

"Are you alright, honey?" my mom asked when she heard my voice.

"I'm fine. Well, I could be better. I just had a crazy dream about Dad. Is he alright?"

"Here. I'll let you talk to him," and with that she put him on the line.

We chatted. He was doing just fine he said. By mid-busy day I had put the dream behind me, but the image of the passenger and Dad's goodbye words remained fixed in my memory.

Time passed – two years to the day. My father died on March 31st, 1993. My beloved dad had taken that last ride in his taxi cab.

He had suffered a massive stroke five days before. We had all camped out in his hospital room for those last long days and nights. We held his hand, talked to him and we said our goodbyes. He could only respond by blinking his eyelids and then even that was lost to him as full paralysis took over his body.

It was only when, left alone with a niece, a nurse herself, as other family members took a much needed trip to the cafeteria, that he died.

"I'm afraid he's gone," she said breathlessly when she came running down the hospital hall to meet us.

"You wouldn't believe it .I know he was totally paralyzed, but he sat right up in bed and reached out as if someone was coming to meet him! It's as if he waited until you were all gone before he left."

In the next few days, my father's spirit 'visited' many family members to say his goodbyes, but those are definitely other stories! It was as if he didn't want to miss anyone.

My father always was a fair-minded man!

TRUISM: "Denial – not a river in Egypt – but a clever device of the ego whose job it is to solve problems and meet challenges. Because the ego hates to be out of work, guess what we have a lot of when it's in charge?" Casandra

AMAZING ADVENTURE #10

FATE AND FORGIVENESS

1992.
This is a true story.

The clicking sound when he turned the ignition key was ominous! I looked over at him with horror. I had a plane to catch. Not wanting to say goodbye to each other, we had left it until the last possible moment to leave.

"You're not going to make your plane." he said quietly.

"Come on back upstairs while I call triple A and we'll figure out what to do."

What to do, I thought. This was a disaster! I would surely get fired from my teaching position if I didn't make it back in time for classes.

We had been having a torrid love affair. The sun and sandy beaches of Florida, an attentive, wealthy man who wanted nothing more than to give me everything I wanted – it had felt like a lush oasis after a desert of marital strife and neglect. I had left an unhappy twenty three year marriage only months before, with no reflection upon why it had failed. I had simply and joyfully bounced right into another man's arms and it was now five months later. Love was the answer I had believed. What the questions should have been I had absolutely no idea!

I paced inside the rented beachfront condo, waiting for the new man in my life to finish calling the auto club. I had met him at a twelve step codependents anonymous meeting just three short weeks after my separation. In my defense, I had come looking for answers. By his own admission, he had come looking for women. What part of his opening statement at the sharing circle had I not heard?

"Hi. I'm here because I am obsessed with work and women."

When it had become obvious he was about to ask me out, my thoughts ran something like this. "Oh, he couldn't really mean what he says. He has been sober now for over two years and he was married for twenty six so he couldn't really have a problem with drinking or women could he?

It's called 'denial'. We believe what we want to believe. And so it was I chose to ignore the group's warning about 'thirteen stepping'! That was what they called dating someone in the program before you had figured out why you were there in the first place.

As my obsession took hold, my children and my work suffered. Every free moment was spent with him at the rented house his ex wife had informed him was his new home.

My daughters were seventeen and twenty two years of age with one away in university and the other one living with me in my matrimonial home. As the weeks went on, it would be more accurate to say, however, that my youngest child lived alone for I was rarely there. My daughters were not pleased with me and thought their mother's behaviour was completely out of character and somewhat disgusting! They were neglected and angry!

Oblivious, I carried on at least until the excesses of our behaviour caught up with me. Deprived of sleep, and not eating properly - living instead on the high of being in love – I eventually crashed.

Seated in my principal's office one day before Christmas vacation, I listened through my sobs as a very traditional Italian man lectured me on my role as a good wife. I was simply to go back to my husband and 'make it work'.

I knew I could no longer 'make it work' with my husband or my job. I was coming unglued! I needed my principal's support to apply for a leave of absence.

He wasn't an unkind man, simply a product of his upbringing, and as my tears continued to flow he saw for himself, I was in no condition to carry on. A leave until the end of the spring break was reluctantly granted.

"You know, you write really well. Your journals are good," he said as he walked toward me. He had just hung up the phone from calling the auto club.

"Where is this going?" I wondered.

True to form he said, "I have a business proposal for you."

Intrigued, I listened as he laid out his plan. He would support me for a year and in return, I would write a book about my life. When it was published, he would own fifty per cent of the rights and royalties. All I had to do now was get an extension on my leave of absence was how he summed up his offer.

Be careful what you wish for. How many of us have said, "I should write a book about my life?' Well, here was my chance.

I looked down at the parking lot at his brand new, shiny red Lincoln Town car and thought. "It's never given any trouble before. Why didn't it start just when I had to leave? Was this meant to be?"

I sucked in a big breath and picked up the phone.

They were not happy with me. To say I came very close to being fired would be an understatement! Completely within their rights to do so, they instead granted my leave.

I sat staring at the blinking cursor on the blank computer screen. What was I going to write? We were back in the dreary spring weather; my new man was once again running his real estate business and I was spending my days at his rented home, staring out a window at his backyard writing whatever 'came through' It was strange. The words seemed to flow through me as if they were coming from another source, but that is another story!

My oldest daughter had just been home for her reading week, but unfortunately I had not been. An obsession is a powerful thing. Because of it, I was able to justify and rationalize my absence.

"My daughters were old enough to look after themselves. They didn't need me." I lied to myself.

Perhaps because, in spite of an unhappy marriage, I had been a loving and involved mother before my temporary bout of present insanity, my oldest daughter had enough courage to challenge me.

We met at the house just as she was coming in and, you guessed it, I was going out.

"Mom, what's going on? You're never here and my sister needs you. I need you! What's happened to you? You're acting like a love sick teenager. It's disgusting! You go to all those meetings, but you sure aren't working your program. You're not walking your talk!"

With that she bolted out of the house, tears streaming down her pretty young face.

Running after her, I grabbed her arm, hoping to wrap her in a hug.

Spinning around, she spit stinging words in my face, "I hate it. I just hate it. I hate you!"

There was no comforting her. She wrenched free, walked over to her car, got in and sped off as I stood on our front lawn, shocked and shaking.

Humbled and horrified, with no one else at home, I went looking for comfort.

Of course the new man in my life assured me my daughter would get over this and that she didn't really mean what she had said.

Of course, I slept there that night and as I lay awake beside his sleeping body. I cried softly, my heart going out to my wounded daughter. My temporary loss of sanity, for indeed I now know that is what an obsession is, had caused her to feel so abandoned in her time of need.

"Please forgive me," I whispered into the still air. "You know I love you more than life itself."

With that, the dim light around me began to change. Soon the room was filled with the most beautiful green glow. It was soft, luminous and seemed to wrap me in an incredible embrace. My heart filled with a sense of love and a peace came over me. I heard her words as if she were in the room speaking them, "I love you so much Mom. I'm so sorry. Forgive me."

Through my tears I watched as the light faded, leaving only the soft glow from the bedside radio. It was eleven in the evening I noted as I drifted peacefully of to sleep feeling secure in my daughter's love.

Several days later, after apologies, we sat together talking and I told her about the strange green glow that had filled the bedroom a few nights before.

"What time was that?" she asked.

When I told her she simply said, "I know. I was surrounding you with healing light."

Interestingly, green is the colour most associated with healing.

TRUISM: "God whispers in your soul and speaks to your heart. Sometimes, when you don't take the time to listen, She has to throw a brick at you!" Casandra

AMAZING ADVENTURE #11

THE FUNERAL FLOWER

1993.
This is a true story.

The coffin was closed at the front of the large room. A portrait of my father, sat atop the casket. Flowers were everywhere. All chairs were filled and all watched as veterans in uniform filed in and respectfully stood near. He was to be given full military honours for he had served with distinction during the Second World War.

All my father's children were there. We had come to say goodbye to a great soul. I had always referred to him as my 'everyday hero' for even as a hard working blue collar man, through difficult financial trials, he had always provided for his family of four daughters. Priceless had been his belief that, even in a 'man's world', his girls were capable of achieving anything they set their minds to. He was known to say, "The cream always rises to the top and dear, you're the cream."

As the minister's words washed over me, I sat reflecting on my parent's life together. I had seen many times the photograph of their wedding day. They were married in the spring of 1946 shortly after war's end. I often suspected I may have been in that photograph as well, as yet undetected!

Mom, even though she had told us wedding attire was very difficult to come by, had still looked radiant in her street length dress, hat, gloves and bridal bouquet with Dad, tall and handsome in his suit, felt fedora and boutonniere standing happily by her side. They appeared to be very much in love.

For forty seven years they built their life together. Always, their home had been a welcoming place. So much so that their children had just kept returning! Week after week, Mom's Sunday roast beef dinners had been a call to gather even after we had married and had children of our own, but those are other stories.

Through it all they had grown up together Mom always said. We were 'kids raising kids'. What she was referring to was the fact that they had both come from difficult homes where emotional issues were not dealt with – ever.

Mom had led Dad into recovery. She, a victim of abuse as a child, had sought help through a twelve step programme and counseling. Dad, a proud and somewhat stubborn man had resisted, until at mid –life, untreated post-traumatic stress from his years of war service had precipitated a breakdown.

A confirmed agnostic up to that point, for as he was fond of saying, he could not believe in a God who would allow war, he began to soften his beliefs. Before the massive stroke which claimed his life at the age of seventy three, he had proven that you can, 'teach an old dog new tricks'!

Becoming an active participant in a spiritual group, he had made new friends, and moved into a place of peace and joyfulness he had never experienced before.

It was just one of those new acquaintances who brushed by me on the sidewalk outside the funeral home.

"That young man knew Dad from his group," my sister said.

I looked over in the direction from which he'd come and saw our mother standing alone, her face ashen. She appeared to be speechless and confused.

"What is it, Mom? What's wrong?" we all asked as we moved protectively around her.

"I've just had the strangest experience;" she said her voice trailing off. "Your father……." She stopped and looked around for a place to sit.

As she settled into a chair, we all noticed she was holding a single flower in her hand.

"Well," she began. "I don't know quite how to tell you girls this. It's somewhat unbelievable, but...." Again her voice trailed off.

By this time we had all found chairs and had pulled them around her as friends walked past giving us some odd looks. The hearse was waiting for us to accompany it, but it was clear our mother needed some time to collect herself.

"Did you see that young man?" she asked. "Well, he was just here and gave me this." She held up the flower for us to see.

"And?" we all said in unison.

She took a big breath and began.

"You know things were hard to come by for our wedding being just after the war and all. Well, I guess I was pretty spoiled, I was only eighteen after all and I wanted my way. Your poor dad, thank goodness he had a few years on me and had the patience of Job! I had insisted that we have flowers and that he wear one. Well, all that was available were carnations and at that time, they had this heavy spicy scent! But they were pink and they went well with my dress so I carried a bouquet of them and your dad agreed to wear one in his lapel. The joke was on me though for being so willful!" She chuckled at the memory.

"All the way through the ceremony your dad did nothing but sneeze!! It turned out he had an allergic reaction to the scent of the carnations! That was such fun, your dad and I laughed about it for years ….." Her voice trailed off again.

In unison our eyes fell to our mother's knee where there lay a single pink carnation.

"He said your father came to him in a dream last night and told him to give me this." She held the flower in her hand.

"He said your father was very specific about what it must be, colour and everything and he was told to give it to me today. His message was simply, 'Give this to my wife. She'll know what it means.'"

Indeed she did.

TRUISM: "Angels are friends who lift us to our feet when our wings have trouble remembering how to fly." Anonymous

AMAZING ADVENTURE #12

A GUARDIAN ANGEL?

1993.
This is a true story.

To say I was stressed would have been an understatement! Looking back, I realize my inability to focus was self induced. I now believe it always is for it's not what happens to us but how we react to what happens that counts.

My mind buzzing with well rehearsed arguments, I was on my way to a court room! The day to face my angry, non compliant separated spouse had finally arrived. Three years into nasty non negotiation, we were about to put the subject of child support before a judge.

Having lived in the suburbs most of my life, I was not familiar, nor comfortable with downtown locations. I may be psychic and able to foretell the future, but figuring out where I am in the present is often another matter! Frankly, I am directionally and spatially challenged.

So it was that I found myself wandering around in an underground parking lot in the vicinity of the courthouse. I could not find my car! Panic filled me as I looked at my watch. I would be late!

As I circled the rows unsuccessfully yet again, I felt the tears welling up! How could I have 'lost' my vehicle? Had it been stolen? It had seemed to just disappear!

Not yet fully spiritually awake and aware, I still believed I had to figure everything out for myself and that life was darned difficult most of the time. Sound familiar?

Our thoughts do create our reality, I now believe, and the universe of course responds in kind. I had been practising 'stinkin' thinkin', and needless to say, as I was often angry and confused, things weren't going that well for me.

Desperate now, I was ready to try anything and so as a last resort it was either call out to the universe for help or crumple into a heap of tears on the cold, concrete floor of the parking lot. I looked heavenward and sent forth my plea.

"Please help me find my car!"

Let's back up a bit here. I have said that I am psychic and I am also a medium who converses regularly with those who have 'crossed over' but, that is now and those are other stories. At this point in time, just beginning to connect with my intuition, I was not convinced enough as yet to put my ego in the back seat and let divine guidance run my life. Well, at least not when things were going well, but now……..

"Help me find my car, please!!" This time I wailed out loud. "I need a guardian angel and I need one now!"

Where he came from I don't know. He seemed to just appear in front of me. Even in my distracted state I thought I would have been aware of someone else's presence in a lonely, deserted underground garage. Women are wired like that.

Dressed in full police uniform, he stood before me and asked, "Can I help you, ma'am?"

Looking back I realize there was something surreal about him. He was young and handsome but his uniform seemed to come from an earlier time – a time when I had read about the brave men who rescued lost kittens and children in the 'Dick and Jane' reader series. It was as if he had stepped off the page as he smiled down at me.

"I can't… find…. my car," I stammered feeling absolutely stupid.

He asked the number of my parking space and when I told him he smiled and said, "Well, there's the problem. You need to be in section 'B' instead of 'A' where you are now."

He went on to explain that the underground lot was divided into two distinct parts, accessible by two different entrances at street level and not connected underground!

I could have been searching forever and never found my vehicle!

"You'll have to go back to street level and use the other underground entrance," he said with a wonderfully warm smile. "Is there anything else I can help you with?" he asked.

"Nooo. Thank you so much." Relief was washing over me. "You've been a wonderful help."

With that he tipped his hat and turned on his heel to leave as I did as well. A few seconds later I turned around for another look and he was nowhere to be seen. He had disappeared as quickly as he had appeared.

Of course, I found my way to my car for I am here writing this story many years later not wandering in a parking lot!! Was he a guardian angel? Who knows? I will tell you what I do know. Now when I need help – I ask. I now am quite in the habit of putting in requests to an intelligence far greater than mine and I am always filled with the same wonderful sense of relief as on that lonely day in the parking lot when the universe moves to support me once again.

Guardian angels, divine providence, God, Jesus, holy spirit, Mother Mary, saints, spirit guides – oh, so many names – oh, so many beliefs, but does it really matter by what name we call upon them?

Perhaps what is important is that we put our ego aside and call upon them at all, but those are other stories!

TRUISM: "You are the CEO of your life." Casandra

AMAZING ADVENTURE #13
WHAT'S IN A NAME?

1993.
This is a true story.

The main character of my novel was beginning to take shape. On leave of absence from my teaching position, I had taken on another vocation – that of author.

Every day I would sit at my keyboard amazed by the words flowing from my mind to the page. It was as if someone else was writing them! At first there seemed no logical order, but over time the passages began to fit together like pieces of a puzzle, each chapter introduced by an original poem, foreshadowing what was to occur next and channeled from my group of spirit guides, 'The Council of One'. I had had no intention of writing any poetry, for this was to be a successful financial venture supported by my new mentor and mate, and poetry didn't exactly fly off book shelves these days.

Nevertheless, the verses came – usually in the quiet moments of the night or early dawn, when my mind ceased creating the prose of my life's story.

What to call myself? That was as yet undecided. Christened Sandra by my parents, for it seemed my father had won the argument of what I was to be called. My mother had come to like the name of the kind lady upstairs and had wanted to name me after her, but my father had been adamant the name would be shortened and he did not want that.

Perhaps some things are just meant to be as my name was shortened and I chose my new name anyway, but that is this story!

Using a combination of my given name and my new man's last name, it formed, what I thought was the perfect name for my character. She would become Casandra spelled with one 's'!

As the writing progressed, I began to identify with my character's name more and more. It was, after all, mainly my story and the name felt like me. As the novel materialized and my divorce finalized, I realized there was no going back. I legally took the new name Casandra for my own. My character would just have to be called something else!

It shook people up when I started using my new name. I really didn't mind the jaw dropped responses I received from family and friends. My business cards printed with my new name, I accompanied my man to many of his business functions. I had become a commercial real estate agent by day, author/ psychic by night! It was a time of extreme challenge, but also great personal growth.

The novel nearing completion, my new name familiar, my post-divorce life settled into a semblance of sanity and routine.

It was a grey spring day and we were attending a real estate symposium, standing chatting with realtors during a break, when a gentleman neither of us knew approached. Taking note of my name tag, he asked bluntly, "Do you know what a Cassandra is?"

Taken aback, we responded that we had no idea. With that he launched into the background of the name. We stood transfixed as the story unfolded.

He explained that in ancient times, the Greeks had laid siege to the walled, wealthy city of Troy. After many unsuccessful months, for the city appeared to be impenetrable, they hit upon an ingenious plan to gain entry.

Appearing to withdraw, the Greeks left behind a 'gift' for the Trojans.

"The Trojan horse!" we both exclaimed at once!

"Yes. The unsuspecting Trojans brought the great structure into their walled city with disastrous results for it was filled with Greek soldiers!"

Everyone knew that part of the story he went on, but did we know that they had been warned of the impending disaster?

The king of Troy's daughter had begged and pleaded with her father and when unsuccessful, had run through the streets of Troy like a mad woman beseeching all not to allow entry of this Greek 'gift'.

They did not listen, and history was written!

"Do you want to know the daughter's name?" he asked.

We still hadn't got the connection and were quite stunned by what followed.

She was called, "Cassandra".

He ended his tale with this final bit of information.

"Actually, there have been many books written about the phenomena. The name has come to stand for a psychic – but one who is not believed! It's referred to as the 'Cassandra Complex' for it has occurred so often throughout history.

With that he turned away leaving me with this final comment.

"I hope you are more fortunate."

A student of numerology, I had understood the power in a name. Each letter is assigned a different vibration and energetically will represent characteristics of the person whose name carries that combination of letters. Numerologists believe that our names are divinely inspired and that there are no accidents in the great scheme of things.

I have always wanted to be heard and believed, perhaps that is why I am a 'Cassandra', but spelled with only one 's'.

Oh yes, the name my mother so passionately felt was to be mine.

You guessed it – Cassandra!

TRUISM: "When asking those who have 'crossed over' if they have a message, it is almost always, 'Lighten up, down there'!" Casandra
Or as they say in AA: "Easy does it!"

AMAZING ADVENTURE #14

"ANOTHER STORY"–THE WINTER FUNERAL

1993.
This is a true story.

The room was filled with silent, expectant people seated around a large board room table in the real estate office. The space was dimly lit, soft breathing the only sound, for it was evening and the business at this time of day was not real estate. I sat at the head of the large oval, mahogany edged table, eyes closed, struggling with what to say.

It was Tuesday evening and our spiritual group, "The Tuesday Night Group" or TNG as we called it (original, weren't we?) had just finished our meditation and now it was time for me, Casandra, the medium/psychic they had come to see and hear to contact my guides, The Council of One, and to answer the many questions of the twenty or so individuals seated around the table.

"I really don't have a specific question to ask. I'd just like to know what you see for me," a young woman began.

With my eyes closed and in a meditative state, I asked her to repeat her name three times so that I might focus on her energy. As she slowly spoke her name I waited for words to stream through my brain. Words that I knew did not come from my thought process, for they landed in my brain as completed concepts, without any inductive or deductive reasoning on my part. It was as if someone else was speaking through me, as if the information was from the individual asking the questions who already knew everything about their own past, present and future and I was able to give voice to that information – information of which they were not consciously aware.

The Council of One spoke through me of the young woman's childhood touching on incidences which had influenced who she was today; foretold a happy love relationship, success at work, and then there was a pause.

"There is a great sadness coming for you." The Council of One paused. "Soon you will lose someone who is very dear to you. We feel it is a young male, perhaps a relative, who will be called to the other side. There is work for him to do there."

"We are looking through his eyes now over a winter landscape. The ground is frozen, a light dusting of snow covers softly rolling hills dotted by barren young trees. The sky is bleak and grey, the mood somber and sad." Their words stopped coming as I struggled to comprehend what I was being 'shown'.

"It's like a military bunker," I said puzzled as I described being inside a concrete structure, built into the side of a hill staring out a horizontal rectangular slit of a window at eye level.

I apologized for what appeared to me to make no sense as my mind raced to find a connection between what I was seeing and the young woman asking the question. Then I remembered what The Council of One had instructed so many times.

"Say what you get just as you receive it!"

So I did. I carried on. I finished with, "This young man appears to be inside this bunker –like structure. He's standing looking out over a winter landscape and he is at peace. All is as it should be.

We are done here. If you have no more questions we will move on to the next person. Peace be with you. "

The evening proceeded with many others asking questions and receiving answers. At its close, the young woman thanked me for all the positive and happy information she had received with no mention of the predicted sadness ahead.

I thought no more about it - until the spring. One Tuesday evening this same young woman arrived at our spiritual group with a relative. It was her aunt she explained who very much wanted to contact someone on the other side. No other details were given.

Her aunt patiently waited her turn, then gave her name and quietly spoke.

"My son Damian was killed in a motorcycle accident Christmas Eve. I want to know if he has a message for me."

Damian had been buried in the winter in an above ground family concrete crypt. It had a 'bunker like' window which looked out over snow covered, rolling hills dotted with barren young trees just as I had seen.

He was twenty-two years of age when he was killed and was the young woman's dearest cousin. They had played together often as children and had been close right up until his death.

There was indeed a message, but that is another story!

**TRUISM : "Suffering is only necessary until you realize it is unnecessary." Eckhart Tolle.
Byron Katie adds, "Suffering is optional."**

AMAZING ADVENTURE #15

DAMIAN AND THE PURPLE PANTS

1994.
This is a true story.

The spiritual group had been meeting now for several months and I was living a double life - commercial real estate agent by day, psychic/medium by night. My ability to scan the body for imbalance and disease, to contact departed loved ones and to predict future events was becoming highly developed with use just as my guides who had identified themselves as 'The Council of One', had predicted. As an aside, I must comment - I thought their choice of a name was somewhat ingenious. How can a council be just one? And the word council, meaning a group, can also, when spelled differently (counsel), refer to guidance, which is exactly what they were giving!

This particular Tuesday a woman in the group was in great emotional pain. Christmas Eve past she had lost her son in a motorcycle accident. The streets of the city had been slick only with a light drizzle, the temperature mild for that time of year. Young, strong, vibrant, full of life, her son had exuberantly taken his new motorcycle out for his first and last ride. Damian had been buried Christmas week leaving his family and friends devastated. His mother, a true skeptic, had only come this night because friends had insisted. I had foreseen this family's tragic loss a few months before - but that is another story.

So it was that as I sat in my calm, altered state ready to answer all questions as quietly she had asked, "Does Damian have a message for me?"

And the answer came. The answer I now sat struggling with, my ego whispering in my ear, "You can't say that! They'll all think you're nuts! It's a ridiculous answer. It makes no sense!"

I drew in a deep breath. I had learned to say what I received just as I received it – in total faith!

Here goes nothing I thought!

"Tell Mom that I don't have to wear the purple pants anymore."

With my eyes closed, I could not see what type of response that got! Damian's energy had more to say so, ridiculous answer or not, I pressed on. He wanted her to know he was happy where he was and very busy. He had been met by two boyhood friends who had also crossed over in the last two years, but that is another story! They were doing great work together on the other side. He asked her not to mourn for him, but to move forward with her life and assured her he would be waiting for her when she crossed over.

I then moved on to others and their many questions and at the end of the evening, as I brought the group back to full consciousness, the discussion and excited chatter began.

Damian's mother was very quiet. Finally, unable to contain my curiosity any longer, I asked, "What's with the purple pants? Did that mean anything to you?"

I think my flippancy was making light of what my ego surely felt had been an unhelpful, inaccurate response.

Quietly, she began.

"I always shopped for Damian's clothes," she said. "Before Christmas, I had bought him a pair of burgundy dress pants. When I showed them to him, he laughingly called them his 'purple pants'. When I was asked to bring clothes for his burial, I took his burgundy dress pants. He was buried in them. Casandra, the casket was only open from the waist up.

No one knew he was wearing his burgundy pants but myself and the undertaker. How could you have known this?"

"Thank you," she continued. "I feel I truly have received a message from my son."

She returned to the group only a few more times, but I heard she began her healing and took her son's advice to move on with her life knowing he was called to the other side, his work here done.

TRUISM: "Success is like a mountain that keeps growing ahead of you as you hike it." George Saunders

"Life is a process, not a goal." Casandra

AMAZING ADVENTURE #16

THE THREE FRIENDS

1994.
This is a true story.

We sat in the now quiet, almost empty boardroom where I had been channeling my spirit guides, 'The Council of One', the room packed this spring night with many who had come seeking answers. One woman in particular had been in deep emotional pain caused by the death of her beloved son Damian, and had asked if he had a message for her. Indeed he had. His words had been given in such a way there could be no doubt who had been speaking - but that is another story!

His mother and his cousin, who had brought her to the group, had stayed behind to talk for it appeared Damian had known he was to meet an early death!

"It all started when he was just a kid." his mother began. "He had these two buddies he hung out with all the time. They were so happy-go- lucky. Nothing much bothered them and they were such good boys! They loved to be out riding their bikes and would be gone for hours into the countryside. They were just happy to be together."

"But after this one bike excursion, they came back different." She continued. "Damian was really quiet which wasn't like him and when I insisted he tell me what was wrong all he said was, 'I swore to the others I would never talk about it, Mom.'

He never did. At least not to his mother, but his cousin was another matter. To her he told bits and pieces and she began now to tell what she knew.

He said they had stopped their bikes in the middle of a big meadow and were lying in the grass taking a rest. He never gave me anymore detail than to tell me they saw and experienced something – something so incredible there were no words to describe it – and they had made a pact right there to never tell anyone about their experience. They also had sworn that they would always be together even in death.

"Casandra," she paused, and then whispered as if the words were too incredible to speak.

"Damian was the last of the three to go."

All three young men were now dead. Damian's two young friends had passed a year apart and himself a year later.

"Wow," was all I could say. I was thinking back to the reading I had just done. Damian had said he had crossed over because there was work for him to do on the other side and he and his two friends were very happy and very busy!

I had not known of the death of the two young boys until now!

Why had three young individuals forged a secret pact to leave this earth within months of one another? Why had they been, 'called home' as Damian said?

I only wish that was another story, but not all knowledge is revealed, not even to psychics!

TRUISM: "Mastering others is the false power of the ego. Mastering the self is true power." Casandra

AMAZING ADVENTURE #17

THE FACE OF EVIL

1994.
This is a true story.

It was so incredibly beautiful! In my mind's eye, I leaned in further. Deeper into the dark pit I peered. My thoughts seemed to stop, my body weaken, go limp, as a thrill of giving over ran through it.

"Submit and be reborn. Fall into me," a voice seemed to rumble up from the dark depths. I wavered. I lingered. I wanted more.

"How seductive," I heard myself think, and with that the spell was broken. A saving shiver of recognition had rippled through me. A gasp of air rattled my lungs, my body stiffened and straightened as I came back into myself. It was not the first time I had been invited to 'fall into the dark side', but that is another story!

My eyes still closed, my body seated in my chair, twenty pairs of eyes transfixed upon me, I heard the room collectively exhale.

It was Tuesday night, the regular gathering of our spiritual group. The 'Council of One', my channeled spirit guides, had answered questions asked by the group when abruptly had come a request by new member.

Bluntly she had asked, "How much to do an exorcism?"

Stunned silence followed. This was new!

Sensing our unease, hurriedly she went on.

"Would you consider driving to the other side of the city to an old farm house where many disturbing events had been taking place?" she asked.

A new owner of the property, she was very disturbed by unexplained flashes of movement and recurring sounds of footsteps throughout the old two story house, but most upsetting, she stated, was that her pets were mysteriously disappearing! In her search for them she had stumbled upon an overgrown part of the yard which emitted a horrific, unexplained odour! A stench was how she put it.

Selling the property was not an option she informed me so that was why she was here. If she couldn't leave, then the spirits had to!

My answer came immediately and surprised even me!

"There's no need to drive all that way. We can do the exorcism right here."

I had slipped back into a trance state.

I 'saw' myself walking over her property. Unkempt and overgrown, the house in need of repair, my conscious mind couldn't help but think that horror movies did get the setting right!

"Your property is a portal". The Council's words boomed out of my mouth.

They spoke with great authority and some frustration as if this subject were one with which they had little patience.

"Spirits use it to exit and enter from other dimensions. Many of them enjoy upsetting and frightening others, but they cannot harm souls here. As with all evil, they have power only derived from the energy of belief, but your beloved pets have been frightened away."

The Council went on. "You will need to search your property for an abandoned well. It is boarded over, overgrown and is the source of the stench. That is the portal. You have the power to close it. Go to the well. Bring others of like mind for there is strength in numbers. Encircle the opening and command the spirits to return to the light. Inform them they are dead, for some do not know it. With the power of your words they will understand they no longer need to feed upon the energy of fear, but instead will seek the Source! Your belief in your power to do so is all that is needed."

With that the Council's energy left and I opened my eyes to the staring faces before me and I couldn't help but think, "Is it really that simple? Withdraw the energy of belief? That was it? Believe instead in the power of our own words to command?"

Who are we anyway I wondered out loud? Then words of scripture came to mind and as I uttered softly, *'Ye are gods and whatever works I have done, ye also may do and even greater things!'* I watched as those seated around me nodded their heads in silent agreement.

"Wow," was my last word that night.

TRUISM: "Rise and shine or rise and whine!" Casandra

AMAZING ADVENTURE #18

TODD AND THE TOWER

1990's.
This is a true story.

Todd looked like a tower. Tall and lean, his long arms and legs supported a lanky body topped by a tangle of dirty blonde hair. He was the young twenty something son of a friend, who in the childhood house next to mine, had suffered abuse from a devoutly religious, sexually deviant father. But that is another story.

In my forties, often giving psychic readings for my friends, my phone would ring late at night and it would be Todd's mother, well into her cups, slurring her words, telling me of the latest drama in her life and asking for guidance. Hopefully, I would give what I believed to be wise advice and hang up the phone only to marvel at how she seemed to lurch from one crisis to the next. It was only years later that I realized that some souls, even with the knowledge given to them of how to be different, lack the courage or the desire to change. It appeared she was not about to give up her red wine or her whine just yet!

At least not until her son Todd took the plunge! Sometimes I think our children come to teach us about life – not the other way around!

"Casandra, can you come with me? I need you!" was how she began the call.

She went on to tell me that Todd was in the hospital with burns over eighty per cent of his body and was not expected to live.

"What happened?" was all I could stammer as I gripped the phone closer to my ear.

The story was sordid yet predictable. All I could think was, "What a waste - such a beautiful young man."

Todd, handsome, a talented musician, with his whole life before him, had no belief in himself. Just as his alcoholic father had, he chose to spend much of his time drunk and in the company of others with no more awareness or ambition than he himself had.

Outside the apartment where Todd and his two drinking buddies lived, the hydro tower had beckoned. They would sit, drink in hand, and discuss how easy it would be to cross the street, scale the fences which contained the tall power towers and climb one.

After weeks of boozy discussion, they concluded it would not be an easy task, but possible and the planning and boasting came to an end.

Late that summer evening, as they sat beer in hand, on their small outdoor patio, gazing up at the stars, it was decided. Tonight was the night! Barely able to walk, staggering, laughing, they headed for the field and the tower. It was late. No one was around, as they climbed the fence, navigated the barbed wire, with only a few cuts and scrapes and landed on the ground inside the compound. Exhilarated by this success, they began their ascent!

Did the alcohol wear off or did exhaustion set in as both of Todd's buddies began to think better of their plan and only half way up, decided to stop and take stock? They watched Todd, as if possessed, continue to climb, deaf to their demands to stop.

Quietly they began their descent and then, firmly on the ground, stood, necks craning to watch Todd continue to scale the tower. He never looked down, his quest ever upward. As they watched him near the top, suddenly the night sky lit up, sparks shooting off his body, and then came a sickening thud as his limp, lifeless form hit the ground.

More dizzying lights, sirens, ambulances, fire trucks, police, all blurred together in a scene of chaos as Todd was transported to hospital.

It was there I saw him. His mother and I, gowned and masked, had been ushered into the sealed and darkened room of the intensive care burn unit, where he lay, wrapped like a mummy, white gauze bandages from head to foot. The machinery keeping him alive whispered and whirred in the background, tubes led in and out of his motionless body. Soft filtered golden light filled the room and as I moved closer and gazed at his form. I sensed his bed was surrounded by row upon row of angelic beings.

"He's in a coma, Cas. They don't think he's gonna make it, but I've been praying so hard for him. I can't lose him." His mother was sobbing.

"I know now how much I've failed him. I just need a second chance! Dear God, I need another chance with him. I know you can reach him. I know you can get through to him, Cas. Let him know I'm here waiting for him," her words trailed off.

I had remained, hand on his bed, standing by his heavily bandaged face, following the peaceful rhythm of his breathing, closing my eyes and going within, only hearing her words as if far, far away. His mother moved to the other side of the room sensing perhaps that her fearful energy would not assist any connection I was trying to make.

Telepathically, he 'spoke' to me in the same voice I knew, his words clear and filled with compassion for his mother's suffering.

"I wanted to go," he said. "But now I'm here, I see things so much more clearly! I see what a gift life is and please tell Mom I always knew she loved me. I can see everything from here. It's so beautiful! I want to stay, but I can see a tiny speck of white light far, far away and I know that it's Mom's light and it's so small, so alone, so surrounded by darkness, I know I can't leave her. Tell her I'm coming back to her. Tell her not to lose faith. I'll be back!"

I did and he did!

The doctor's were astounded by his rapid healing and recovery. What was even more unbelievable was the lack of scaring on his beautiful young body.

Many, many people had been asked to pray for Todd and I am convinced because of that legions of angelic healers had been drawn to his bedside.

Todd had seen life was truly a gift and that to remain fully present, free of addictions and compulsions, was a daily demonstration of gratitude.

TRUISM: "If you can't be a good example, then you'll just have to be a horrible warning!" Catherine Aird

"There are no victims, just volunteers." Casandra

AMAZING ADVENTURE #19

THE COMA CONNECTION

1990's.
This is a true story.

Looking back, I know I have contributed to raising two wonderful women – one who is a teacher and dedicated to helping children here in Canada and one who is now working as a veterinary assistant/missionary in the slums of South Africa, helping both children and animals. Perhaps it was always in them to be who they are, for in this story is evidence of early altruism.

My oldest daughter, who is now the teacher I spoke of, was just a teenager when this story began. Always a hard worker, she was looking for a part time job which would allow her to have experience in her chosen field of social work. Her choice of a teaching career would come later, for at this point, having witnessed my life as an educator, she had decided teaching was too demanding - as if social work was not! Ah, the blind vision of youth!

A relative, who owned and operated a head injury clinic, suggested she had the perfect position for her. A client, whose son had been seriously injured in an automobile accident, was now a quadriplegic who needed a weekend caregiver.

We discussed how demanding the work would be, but she was determined especially after meeting the young man and learning his story.

His name was Jules and he looked like he could have stepped from the pages of Roman history. Dark of eye and skin, with a long straight aquiline nose and curls about his face, he was strikingly handsome. At this point, he had neither speech nor movement of his body below his neck. He spent his time either in a bed or wheelchair.

But oh his eyes – how they followed the girls everywhere! In no time he was in half in love with my pretty, young daughter. That was obvious to all who saw them together. And why shouldn't he be? Devastatingly injured at a time when he had been just beginning his adult life, he had never had a chance to court, love, or marry the woman of his dreams.

No one knew why such a tragedy had occurred. All we had was how.

At the family's country place for the weekend, he had taken the truck on an errand. He had stopped at the intersection, obeying the sign, but the driver of the truck coming the other way, had not. It was argued later that an overgrowth of brush had obscured the stop sign from the truck driver's view, but the courts settled in Jule's favour. There had been no doubt; a young life had been unalterably changed due to negligence.

Unconscious when his limp body was pulled from the wreckage, he was to stay that way for many months. In a deep coma, on life support, the doctors held out little hope of a recovery. Faithfully his father visited almost everyday. A tenacious man, he never gave up hope and always talked about his son as if he were fully recovered.

Jules shared a hospital room with another young man who was also in a coma. The nurses would come in and joke with his father saying that his name really suited him. Known as the father with the big heart, he was always referred to by his last name, Mr. Hart! He was not a relative as it is a common name, if not a common condition!

After several months of visits, with no improvement, doctors were suggesting they take Jule's off life support. His father refused.

Then, when all seemed hopeless, it happened.

Walking down the hall to his son's room one day, he encountered a young man in a wheelchair who looked very familiar. Looking again, he realized it was the same young man who had shared a room with his son these many months. He stared amazed as it dawned upon him that the young man now beaming up at him was fully conscious and about to speak to him!

"Hi, Mr. Hart," he said cheerfully. "I have a message for you from Jules. He says he's coming back. Give him time. He's coming back! Oh, and he loves you, you know."

Thunderstruck, all Jule's father could do was nod, smile and watch as the now recovered young man was wheeled away by his attendant.

Jules did indeed wake up weeks later just as the other young man had foretold and that is how my daughter came to be his caregiver and learn of his incredible story.

He has recovered sufficiently now to live in his own home, a semi-independent young man, assisted by caregivers and modern technologies so that he can speak and get around. He has never courted nor married, but perhaps that was not his destiny in this life. .

After several years as his part time caregiver, my daughter went on to graduate and live her own life and Jules, as tenacious as his father, did fulfill a promise he made to her.

As he would struggle valiantly to lift himself out of his wheelchair and take a few steps, my lovely daughter would clap her hands in delight and say to him, "Jules you're doing so well, promise me one day you'll dance at my wedding!!"

He never gave up and with some assistance, beaming from ear to ear; he did indeed dance with the bride.

It was never revealed to me why he chose to return to a body that stubbornly still limits him, but perhaps one day that will be another story!

TRUISM: "Every time you argue with reality, you lose." Byron Katie

"It is what it is." Casandra

AMAZING ADVENTURE #20

SNAKES IN THE STREETS!

1997.
This is a true story.

The Council of One was very busy! At least I was calling upon them for guidance a great deal. Our Tuesday night meetings were going well. Usually twenty to thirty people would crowd into our boardroom to hear predictions and ask for personal guidance.

We were publishing a newsletter entitled, "The Answer Within", for I truly believed, even though clients came seeking psychic guidance, they carried their answers within them.

There was a lot of fear in the group these days. Speculation regarding the dawning of a 'new age' was rampant. End of the world scenarios were talked about as the new millennium approached. Many recited the ancient predictions of natural disasters, global devastation and the ending of the Hopi Indian calendar at 2012! So it was that on this particular night the question came.

"Casandra, will you ask the Council of One what natural disasters they see on our planet in the next decade? Will we be safe here?"

I had been sitting at the head of the large board room table, eyes closed, breathing deeply in a light trance and only moving to turn my head to the questioner.

In response, a brief flash of an otherworldly room, bathed in golden hued white light, with wise, white haired learned looking beings robed in long flowing gowns bending over a huge table laden with golden scrolls and maps came to me.

That scene faded, and I was thrust into the fury of nature's devastation. Sheer terror choked me. I felt the fight for life of those involved.

People were running, screaming, searching for higher ground, climbing up and being blown out of trees. Palms were bent and uprooted, their fronds sweeping the salt seawater soaked earth. Screams rang in my ears; tears flowed on my face as I recounted what I was seeing. The massive moving wall of water was swallowing up the land and the inhabitants of the Indonesian arc of islands, many never to appear again. An open map of Indonesia on the table before the wise ones flashed before my eyes and came their words, "You will be safe for it is here."

Calmly, compassionately, their words continued to flow through me.

"There will be great devastation, great loss of life. No ground will be high enough for escape. Thousands will drown. The sea will claim its own."

The voice of the Council went on in a new tone now. There was a trace of irritation, but mostly sadness, disappointment and frustration.

"You on earth must change your ways. This event heralds a time of much upheaval, a coming to the beginning of end times. Yet, we have great hope for humanity as the balance in the collective consciousness is shifting. There is more awakening, more enlightenment. This can be the dawning of the new beginning."

"Take heed. When the snakes are in the streets, it is near."

With that their energy left me and I opened my eyes to see the open mouthed faces around me.

"Wow! That was really something! Are you alright, Casandra? You seemed really upset."

There was a buzz of excited discussion, and then the session ended. A little dazed, we all left for the evening wondering when the predicted event would occur.

The years went on. Our lives went on. Indonesia went on.

In the fall of 2003, one Sunday as I read the Toronto Star newspaper a small story in the travel section caught my eye.

It was titled, "Snakes in the Streets of Indonesia" and told of the problem of poisonous snakes coming to higher ground in the cities and villages.

"Well,…" I mused. "Could it be?"

One thing I did know about information from the 'other side' was that their sense of timing was not like ours. Seven years was just a hiccup to them.

The Indonesian Tsunami hit on Dec. 26th, 2004 with no warning. Over a quarter of a million people lost their lives and some of the land is still submerged.

I was safe.

TRUISM: "The definition of insanity is doing the same thing over and over again and expecting a different result. Nothing changes, if nothing changes!" Alcoholics Anonymous

AMAZING ADVENTURE #21

DENNIS AND THE DOG

2000.
This is a true story.

I had a sister who moved to Ireland to follow her dream. It was summer vacation, my grown daughter wished to spend more time with me, my sister wanted to see us, so what could more wonderful than booking two flights to Dublin?

The south of Ireland is beautifully lush and green just as they say! My sister Colleen -I know how Irish that sounds – I didn't make it up – that is truly her name - had rented a cottage perched on a cliff overlooking the ocean, with sheep and lamb grazing on the hillsides and the sea spray filling the air. There was always a mist about – even when it wasn't raining, it was misting. The locals called it, 'going soft'. That was an expression which raised a few tourists' eyebrows - especially when a gentleman gave it as an answer to the question, "How are things?"

And it was the scariest place in the world to drive! Not only were they on the other side of the road, but when there was a road in this remote village - it was one way! With squat but very sturdy stone walls lining the sides that meant there was only one thing to do when meeting another car - stare it down until it backed up or back up yourself!

I also could never get warm! The damp ate right into your bones – even in August. We met a young man at a local pub who had just returned from a visit to Canada and had told us that visit was the first time in his twenty-two years that he had been warm! Canada, warm?

I must admit my sister handled these situations with aplomb – she was in love with an Irishman and I think that had something to do with her affection for this beautiful, but barren and bleak coast.

The rented cottage was rustic, rundown chic. At least when Colleen got finished with it –she added the chic! An artist, she had splashed the walls with warm, welcoming colour, arranged plump cushions and draped cozy throws across the overstuffed chairs. The rooms she filled with the smell of herbs and spices and she always lit a crackling fire and brewed a hot pot of tea when we returned from our jaunts!

It was as we returned from one of those jaunts, once again greeted by the black and white border collie that had seemed to take up residence in her driveway, I had to ask, "Did you get a dog?"

"Oh, that's just Duke." she said matter-of-factly. "He came with the house."

"Does he ever come inside? Do you feed him? Who does he belong to?" I asked. I like to nail things down.

"He belonged to the former owner who passed away. He won't leave. I do feed him occasionally, but I really don't want to encourage him to stay. I'm sure he'll eventually wander off to a new home." With that she felt the matter was closed. She doesn't have my same compulsive need to 'nail things down'.

"But, doesn't he get cold at night?" I asked. Was there a little bit of projection going on here? I was cold at night!

"Oh, for goodness sake, Sis, he's a border collie. He's born and bred for this climate. No one keeps their dogs inside here. They are working animals! They herd the sheep. That's what they do!" she said somewhat exasperated.

I think she worried about the dog's welfare probably as much or more than I did, but being new to the area, felt somewhat overwhelmed and helpless to change the situation she had inherited.

My lovely grown daughter, who makes her living as a veterinary technician saving the animals of the world, and is the most pragmatic, level headed person I know, having overheard our conversation, hoisted a bag of groceries off the 'bonnet' of the car and said, "He'll be fine. I've been feeding him. Let's make dinner. I'm starved!"

So it was each day we were greeted lovingly by Duke in the driveway and every night, around two a.m., startled awake by Duke howling at the sky. He was there and he was on watch.

One afternoon while serving tea, my sister casually stated, "The neighbours say this place is haunted, you know. That's why the rent was so reasonable. Nobody wanted to live here." Colleen had a way of dropping conversational bombs!

"Fascinating," I thought. "Wonder why I haven't felt any evidence of a presence. I guess I'm too busy trying to stay warm!"

We were all snuggled up in the living room this evening, sipping our tea, when my daughter went upstairs to the bathroom. It was at the end of a long hallway, the doorway backlit by moonlight from an upstairs window which looked out over the yard and driveway.

She didn't seem to be gone very long and when she returned she sat down almost on my lap! She snuggled into me, wrapping her arm in mine and didn't say a word. Because this demonstrably affectionate behavior was somewhat out of character for her, I looked down at her face buried in my voluminous Irish sweater.

She was absolutely ashen!

"You're as white as a ghost! Did you see one just now?' I joked.

"What'd the guy look like who lived here before?' she asked, her voice shaky.

"You mean, Dennis, the guy who died?" Colleen asked.

"Yes. Was he tall and thin with scraggy grey hair? Did he wear pants with suspenders and plaid shirts?"

"That certainly sounds like the fellow they described to me. He apparently died in bed upstairs." Colleen answered.

"Well. I just saw him," my daughter said quietly. "He was standing in the doorway of the bathroom. I could see him from the end of the hall."

"Did he say or do anything?" we asked incredulously in unison.

"No. He looked at me like he wondered who I was and then the image just faded away."

"Well, two things to do," I said. "Take you to the bathroom and then hold a séance!"

And that's just what we did. We gathered around the kitchen table that night. We lit three candles – representing past, present and future. We held hands and we prayed, calling upon the energy of love and light to surround, enfold and protect us and then we spoke out loud to Dennis.

We told him he was dead and that it was his time to go to the light. We assured him he would be met with love and loved ones and that there was nothing left to hold him to this place. His time here was done.

We blessed him. We blessed the house. We blessed one another. We blew out our candles and went calmly to bed.

It seemed we slept more soundly that night and as we gathered around the kitchen table for our morning meal, we looked at one another and said in unison.

"He's gone isn't he?"

"Yes," we agreed. Dennis' energy was no longer with us. And so it seemed was Duke. Our loyal black and white border collie never returned to our driveway or to howl at our night sky again.

There was no need. His master was gone to a new home - one which needed no protection.

TRUISM: "When it comes to relationships, ladies, ask for what you want. Let us be clear on this one. Subtle hints do not work. Strong hints do not work. Obvious hints do not work. Just say it!" Casandra

AMAZING ADVENTURE #22
THE DAISIES

2001.
This is a true story.

I have a dear friend – she is part of a group of women whom I named the, 'Aluminum Azaleas'. We are not quite as strong and formidable as the 'Steel Magnolias' as yet. As so many of us have, our group has steadfastly been there for one another through many of life's trials - divorce, job loss, cancer, cheating husbands to even the death of a grandchild, we have held each other close, listened and wept with and for one another.

Often I was asked to practice my psychic abilities for my friends and one in particular, in the fall of 2001, seemed to need my help. The love of her life, was not feeling well.

"Can you do one of those 'body scans' you do?", she asked.

Only needing his name, I 'felt' his energy and scanned over his body.

"I see a dark spot on his liver. I don't want to scare you, but I think he should have it checked and soon!" From past readings I knew black areas on the body signified a blockage of energy which meant cancer.

Many of my 'insights' about my friend and her family had been very accurate in the past so she wasted no time dragging a somewhat unbelieving husband to the doctor's office.

The resulting tests were 'inconclusive'. There had been a shadow on the liver in the scan, but it appeared cloudy. It was decided to adopt a 'wait and see' protocol. Come back in the spring for more tests he was told.

Sadly, it was too late by then. The undiagnosed cancer had grown dramatically and her beloved husband, in the spring of the year, died in the home he cherished, surrounded by those he loved. Though devastated, with the help of family, friends and wonderful neighbours she carried on as best she could. One of those wonderful neighbours came to help out with her gardens several weeks after the funeral. Before her husband had become ill, my friend had hinted she would like the daisies in their garden moved under her kitchen window, but her husband hadn't thought it a priority so consequently had done nothing. The neighbour had known about the discussion, and in an attempt to cheer her up after her loss, had taken it upon himself to move the now blooming daisies under the kitchen window where she would be able to look out at them.

Shortly afterward, still in deep pain over the loss of her husband, she had asked me to come to the house to see if I could 'contact' his spirit. Was he alright? Was he in a good place? Was he happy and was he watching over her she wanted to know?

We had never discussed the issue of the daisies, so when his voice came through with his greeting, I repeated what I heard even though it seemed to make no sense to me and appeared to be an inconsequential remark.

After hundreds of psychic readings, I have learned I should never question what I am given, but rather, in complete faith, say it exactly as it's received!

Here goes I thought to myself as I repeated exactly what had come through.

"I like the daisies under the kitchen window. You were right to suggest it. It's the perfect spot for them."

There was a sharp intake of breath, silence and then sobs as I continued to give my friend the message that she was indeed loved and watched over every day.

TRUISM: "Forgive. You'll feel better." Casandra

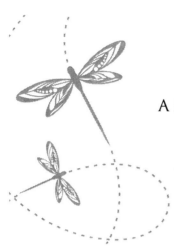

AMAZING ADVENTURE #23
AN OLD STORY

2001.
This is a true story.

As a religious education teacher I have been a student of the Bible for many years. Always, it has amazed me how the essence of every human condition has already been addressed in this inspired collection.

Carl Jung referred to these innate, universal prototypes used to interpret observation, as archetypes - constructs which have arisen through humanity's evolution and are understood by all. There truly is nothing new under the sun and we know it.

Let me offer my humble reason why I think he was on to something. During readings the same symbols come through again and again. They are a universal 'code', often bringing with them an epiphany!

I'm quite sure every woman reading this understands the archetype, 'princess' and every man, 'prince'. The characteristics and roles of each are well understood in our collective minds.

As my intuitive self often speaks to me in such terms during a reading, it was not surprising, when a very familiar bible story came as the answer to a question.

Let me begin this story at the beginning.

My married daughter had just purchased her first home and had invited one of her closest friends to help with some decorating. It seemed like a great idea when after dinner, she said, "Mom, you'll do a reading for us won't you! We want to know when she's going to meet the man of her dreams and how many kids we're both going to have!"

Her mischievous smile seemed to say, "C'mon, Mom. Show us how good you are!"

"No pressure," I thought.

A prophet is never believed in his (her) home town it is said and that had been very much the case with my family. Able to clear a room with a single mention of psychic readings, I had often found myself alone in a crowd. Actually, it had proven useful at times if you get my drift.

Seated around her large oak dining table were my daughter, her new husband, her oldest and dearest friend and myself.

"You will both bear sons!" were the first words of the reading. "They come as twin souls into this world, even though inhabiting different wombs. They have been here together before, born as the ancients Jacob and Esau. Esau was the first twin to emerge and Jacob came into the world holding his heel. The pattern of their lives now will be the same."

With this the reading moved on to other predictions and it was just as well as my conscious mind was already trying to interpret their futures based upon what had been given for I knew the story well.

The reading continued. "I see a tall, handsome man with grey at his temples standing behind you now. He is coming. He will be your husband and father of this son." I said referring to my daughter's friend.

Needless to say, there was excitement in the room as the reading came to an end. As they chatted happily about becoming mothers of sons, I did not share my more ominous interpretation.

An old story full of deception, disobedience and betrayal swirled through my mind.

As a humble student, I will now summarize my understanding of that story.

About two thousand years before the birth of Jesus, Isaac the son of the Hebrew patriarch, Abraham, had twin sons whom he named Esau (red haired first born) and Jacob (heel grabber). The prophecy of their birth had decreed the 'younger shall rule over the elder' In other words, Jacob, the quiet, studious son, should receive the birthright from his father while, Esau, whom Isaac favoured for his abilities as a rugged hunter, would be secondary in power and influence.

When the time came to bestow the blessing, Isaac, giving in to his favouritism, had called for his eldest son Esau.

His wife, quickly covering the smooth skinned Jacob with animal skins, presented her favoured son to receive the blessing. Almost blind and even doubting the voice was that of Esau, Isaac nevertheless became convinced by the hairiness of Jacob's arm, and believing it to be Esau, bestowed the birthright disobeying the word of God.

Disaster of course struck when the truth was learned. Jacob left the land and the two brothers did not lay eyes upon one another for many years. Both prospered, and Jacob, lead by dreams and God's guidance, made his way back to his brother to make restitution even though he fully expected to meet with violence.

In a surprising twist, Esau was filled with great joy and forgiveness.

Jacob had fathered twelve sons, from who sprang the twelve tribes of Israel while Esau is considered the father the Arabic race.

All this was running through my mind. Was history to repeat itself? Would deception, disobedience and betrayal manifest in the lives of these two sons yet to be born? Would forgiveness and reconciliation once again be the outcome? What did it all mean?

These are questions yet to be answered, for indeed both my daughter and her friend had sons. My daughter's son was born first. Her friend's husband and her son's father was indeed a tall, handsome man with premature grey at his temples.

At the time of this writing, the boys are nine and seven years of age. As for the meaning of the vision, only time will tell. Perhaps that will be another story.

TRUISM: "Why would you believe anything YOU haven't tested for truth?" Casandra

AMAZING ADVENTURE #24
THE BIG SADNESS

Spring 2001.
This is a true story.

I awoke every morning with an incredible heaviness – an all pervading sadness. Its weight stayed with me as I moved through my mornings. I knew it wasn't mine. It didn't come from me. I am a psychic and an empath and feelings of others often run through me like ripples in a pond leaving no after effect. When I do readings, tears will often flow down my cheek as I release others' pain, and I will have little or no memory of what transpired. But this was different. It moved with me throughout my days, unshakeable and heavy. When at rest, no longer distracted by the business of daily life, it would settle in, taking hold. It felt like a big, dark cloud following me everywhere. It was as if everything around me was enveloped in a grey fog. This was bigger than me, I knew that. It was as if the entire country was weeping, mourning a great loss.

Because I knew this pain was not mine, I would put it to the back of my mind, but it did affect my behaviour and often others would ask if anything was wrong. I would hear myself say, "I really don't know. I just know a big sadness is coming."

That word 'know' is powerful. It indicates more than just logical deduction or 'head' knowledge. It is an awareness that comes from your entirety – head, heart, gut. You just 'know'! You don't know how you know, but you just do.

The timing of this great sadness however, I did not know. That's the thing about being psychic. At least, for me, the date of future events is still difficult to predict as is the specific way they will unfold.

I have often reflected upon this. Why is it that predictions are obscure and only in retrospect make sense? Many would argue that meaning is assigned only with hindsight and often I believe that to be true. We are all points of perception; small 't' truth is relative, reflective of the meaning we assign, but I can't help but wonder if some events are predestined. It's as if, before I came into this life, I selected a version of it, much like I would select a recorded movie, one I have viewed before, and I 'know' the plot!

If you are reading this story now twelve years later, I am sure you know what great sadness was coming!

We were all called into the library of our small elementary school this September morning. It was unusual to assemble the entire staff and student body at this time of the day. I led my grade five students into a hushed room where all eyes were focused upon a television screen. The room was deadly quiet. All watched in horror as the scene of an airplane crashing into a tall New York city skyscraper was played over and over again with the harried reporter stating that the air was choked full of mysterious grey ash drifting down from the building and covering everything. He either did not realize what it was or was too horrified to speak the words.

I know now what it was. As a minister I am familiar with cremation.

The rest of the day unfolded as I'm sure many of you remember. Another plane; another tower; the third plane crashing into the pentagon; the unending speculation and horror of witnessing such incomprehensible events!

Why I wondered, had I been able to feel this wave of pain months before it transpired? Was I to do anything with this foreknowledge and if I had been meant to, why had it not been more specific – detailed enough to be useful?

Answers I do not have. I only have my story to tell.

There is a dream that stays with me still. It came months after these events. Perhaps birthed out of the fear of more terrorist attacks, it was one of those dreams that felt prophetic. I only hope I am wrong for in the dream, I am hovering over a downed passenger jet. Upon looking down at the wreckage, my only thought is, "What a mess." I feel great sadness and loss as my eyes sweep over the scene. The tail of the jet is the only part intact - the red logo in full view. Seats, clothing, baggage and bodies are strewn everywhere. It has just happened and no one is moving – anywhere. The plane has crashed in a semi mountainous area, resting precariously on the side of a steep hill. I 'know' it is in the New England area of the United States perhaps on approach to New York City. It was not pilot error nor mechanical failure, but the result of an explosion.

This prediction has yet to come to pass. I still do not fly that airlines My hope is it never becomes another story!

TRUISM: "Often the only roadblock is the block sitting upon your shoulders." Casandra

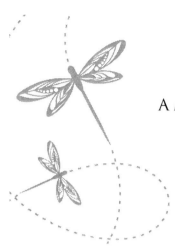

AMAZING ADVENTURE #25

A MOVER AND A SHAKER!

2001.
This is a true story.

I have always been fascinated by cute little girls with curly blonde hair! You know the kind you see in the Norman Rockwell paintings — plump rosy cheeks, that glint of mischief in their eye as they sit primly in their starched pinafores. Perhaps my fascination was because I was never that idyllic image! A scrawny child, with long straight legs, it was also my misfortune to have inherited thin, straight hair! My mother would often comment, "Straight as a poker- that's the hair in the Hare family!" (Our surname was Hare!) There was not a curl in sight!

So it was that my persistent hope for a cherub of a grandchild crowned with a head of strawberry blonde curls was somewhat laughable! But there she was! At least the image I 'saw' every time I looked at the stairs winding their way up to the second floor of my daughter's home. There she would be, her smiling rosy cheeked faced surrounded by strawberry blonde curls!

My oldest daughter had been married for some time now and of course there was talk of grandchildren. I had always 'known' I would have a grandson, but that's another story.

It was late spring and many of our family were gathered on the front porch of my daughter's home. I don't remember what the occasion was, but our family didn't usually need one to get together! Involved in the conversation, I wasn't quite sure I had heard her last statement correctly.

"Give Grandma another cup of tea," was what I had thought she said. She was looking directly at me!

My thoughts tumbled over themselves. Did she mean me? A grandma-that only meant one thing -she was expecting!

They all laughed as they watched me finally 'get it'!

"Wow!" was all I managed before the tears and the hugs! As this was to be the first grandchild as well as the first great grandchild it was cause for celebration!

Of course the questions then flowed.

"When?" and "Do you know what sex it is?"

"April" and "No", were the answers.

The early months of waiting passed. Thanks to wonderful new technology, my daughter was able to tell me it was to be a granddaughter! I must confess there was a brief thought that oh, I guess my prediction was wrong. I had been convinced I was to have a grandson! I was, but not as my first grandchild!

As the birth date approached, I couldn't resist. I would have to go and 'meet' my soon to arrive grandchild! Now, you might ask how I proposed to do that. Let's just say I had 'connections'!

If I focused on the energy of the soul inhabiting my daughter's womb, I believed, I would be able to receive a message.

Seated comfortably in my own rocking chair, eyes closed, miles away, I lovingly focused on my daughter and the new life growing inside her.

"Grandma, I'm gifted you know!' came this small child's voice. It bubbled excitedly on. "I'm going to be a real mover and shaker too! I might get in my own way sometimes, but that's okay. See you soon. Oh ya, I'm a girl!"

With that the energy left me. A happy giggle echoed through the room and a wide smile spread over my face.

Gifted-wow! Having been a school teacher for many years, observing many students struggles to master the curriculum, it was pleasant to think of my granddaughter having the necessary brain power to make life somewhat easier. As for the part about getting in her own way, large egos and stubbornness seemed to be part of our genetic family lottery so that came as no surprise.

What did come as a surprise was her appearance when she finally presented herself. Weighing in at almost ten pounds, she was definitely cherubic, but though her hair was fair there was very little of it! Where were the curls, I wondered?

As I sit now staring at a photo of my rosy cheeked granddaughter taken when she was nearing two years of age, there are indeed strawberry blonde curls surrounding her face! Perhaps no surprise, as I was to later find out, her father, were it not for his athletic buzz cut, would be sporting black curls! Who knew?

Now in the fourth grade, with standardized tests behind her, she is officially considered 'gifted'. We knew.

As for being a 'mover and shaker', she is only nine years old, but the signs are there! Remember that mischievous look in the eye of the little curly headed cherub seated on the stairs? I can hardly wait to see what she does with her curls and her gifts.

TRUISM: "Women get psychic as they age. You never have to confess your sins to a woman over fifty. They always know." Andy Rooney

AMAZING ADVENTURE #26

STABBED IN THE BACK!

2003.
This is a true story.

I love the sea - the smell of it, the sound of it! Perhaps I was a sailor in a past life –who knows, but I am never happier than when I am onboard a ship!

Retired from teaching, I was now fulfilling a dream- at least most of it! A month on a cruise ship sailing to port after port in the Mediterranean and then four days of open sea as we crossed the Atlantic Ocean to dock in Fort Lauderdale, Florida, was my idea of heaven on earth! I only wished the man in my life had chosen to come along. Instead he had suggested I take my mother and even though she and I were great friends and having fun, I missed his company.

My new man and I had been together now for over twelve years and he had remained 'clean and sober' throughout that time. Attending twelve step meetings after my separation from my husband, we had become guilty of what the group called, 'thirteen stepping'! That is, dating someone in the program before you had completely worked through or resolved why you were there in the first place!

Never chemically addicted, my issue had been co-dependency. Under the illusion I could 'fix' other people, I had spent twenty three years trying to change my first husband, but that is another story!

My new man had been a heavy drinker, smoker and workaholic. After twenty six years of building a successful real estate empire together, his wife had had enough. One of her complaints was his insistence on a yearly allotment of a quarter of a million dollars which he felt entitled to 'invest' in risky commodities trading. Always after the 'big score', he had 'invested' away over a million dollars of the money she had worked hard to earn while they were together. Tired of constant work, the dysfunctional family systems which made up their staff and his refusal to change, she had left.

There is a reason, the old timers in the twelve step program counsel against getting romantically involved! They know that when you are in recovery 'your ears are often stuffed with cotton' and your head convinced you really don't need to be at meetings because 'you are not as sick as the rest of them'! Ego is usually still rampantly running your show!

Perhaps that is why I didn't 'hear' when he would share weekly that he was afraid he'd go bankrupt and that he was obsessed with women!

No, I chose to 'see' that he appeared to being doing very well financially, that he could and did help me out by moving into my house and paying rent and that he was in love with only me!

To his credit, we did have many wonderful years together. He was a terrific step father to my daughters, loving, generous and easy to be around. Perhaps that is why I didn't see any harm in the occasional trip to the casino. He taught me to play blackjack and shoot craps and it was great fun at first. Fun, except when I would stand behind him at the blackjack table with large amounts riding on a single bet! He was lucky —most of the time - and managed to finance our jaunts to the casino and still keep his 'gambling stash' intact.

When my logical mind asked what was the point of continuing to gamble if the best you could hope for was to break even, he laughed and said, "That's not the point! It's the thrill of the chase!"

Funny, I always felt a little ill after one of his gambling sessions. It certainly didn't do it for me. I worked too hard for my money to understand the thrill of risking it!

Next there were the reams and reams of paper piled high in the home office. Commodity charts – he was trading again! This time, he said it was just on paper. He was practising, honing his skills for when the real estate company was profitable enough to engage in trading once again.

When the student is ready, the teacher appears. What part of this freight train of a lesson did I not 'see' coming? Simple answer - none of it, but it was time!

The rocking and bumping of the cruise ship woke me. We were docking. Today was to be a day of sightseeing in glorious Ville France. Rolling over to get out of my single bunk, I felt it. A pain shot through my mid back so severely that I fell back onto the bed! I had had back problems in the past but always in the lower region. This was new. The pain was squarely between my shoulder blades.

"Mom," I groaned. "I'm going to need some help to get out of bed!"

We managed to roll me out of the bunk and get me seated in a chair. The pain was excruciating. I spent the day on pain pills with cold packs and a massage. It did get better after a few days, but it left me wondering what I had done to bring on such a violent and sudden attack.

At the end of November, mom and I returned home. Christmas came and went, I chugged along in my relationship, but I did notice we were spending more and more time apart. I was involved with my married daughter and her small family and often spent the weekends in the small town where she and my mother and two sisters now lived. He often preferred to stay in the city. On one particular time in the spring while I was away, I had tried unsuccessfully to reach him at home. He had spent the weekend alone at a local casino resort he informed me on my return. I thought it a bit strange, but there was that denial again! It certainly isn't a 'river in Egypt', but a powerful coping mechanism. I was not quite ready yet to face the truth of our lives.

It was becoming evident I did not have a companion with whom to share my retirement. He spent hours on his computer and when he wasn't doing that, planning his television viewing as if it were a matter of life and death that he keep his mind occupied. We would joke about his 'couch potato' lifestyle. I kept busy with other things, but I missed his presence in our life. His mind so often seemed to be elsewhere. Now, I know his obsessive behaviors and addictions were an attempt to manage his cycles of mania and depression.

One Sunday evening in late summer, just as we had finished a lovely dinner he predictably left the table to log onto his computer. When I put my arms around his neck and literally begged him to come and watch a movie with me, he abruptly clicked to another screen, made some excuse about what he had to do and brushed off my overture.

Wounded, I walked into the solarium of our high rise condominium where our floor to ceiling windows looked out over the city's night sky. As the lights twinkled before me, I looked into the darkness and said in a whispered voice, "Dear God, help me. I can't do this any more. I'm done."

The next morning when I logged onto our home computer I saw a minimized box flashing at the bottom of the screen. He obviously had neglected to exit completely from the site he had been using.

With a simple click my life changed. My prayer heard and answered, my world turned upside down. There in front of me was Ashley Madison's site inviting my man, my lover, to contact women in his area who were interested in having discreet extra marital affairs. He had a code name and reading further, I discovered he had been contacting several of these willing women.

Hands shaking, I dialed his office number.

"What am I looking at?" I asked. I described the site.

There was a groan on the other end of the line. "If I tell you it could destroy us," he answered.

"Come home," was my reply.

The whole sordid tale came out as he sat across the room from me, hands behind his head, his body sprawled casually back against his chair, coolly explaining the how and why as if he were presenting a business proposal.

He had been lonely while I was away on the cruise he said. A month was just too long was his excuse. He had needed to have sex so he had called an escort service and it turned out he liked it. It was thrilling to be with someone exciting and new! He had continued to see girls even after I had come home taking one away gambling the weekend I had been unable to reach him.

"You need to leave now," I said flatly. "Pack your bags and get out."

I had clicked on the Ashley Madison site at nine thirty that morning and by three thirty in the afternoon I was alone, single once again.

It was only months later, when scrolling through the call log of our telephone, I came across the name of a company I did not recognize. When I investigated, I discovered it was an escort service. The date of the call was the same day I had awakened thousands of miles away in the middle of the Mediterranean Sea with an excruciating, unexplained pain in my back - coincidence? Or is there a reason we refer to betrayal as being, 'stabbed in the back'?

I now realize that my beloved friend was very ill, suffering from a manic high, incapable of making good decisions. Nevertheless, he refused to seek treatment and over the course of the next three years did indeed bring about the one thing he feared most - personal bankruptcy. He now lives above a donut shop with a male roommate spending his time smoking and gambling online when he has the money to do so. He claims to be happy and perhaps he is, but there is great sadness in his eyes when he holds my hand and says simply, "I'm so sorry. I just messed up."

TRUISM: "Don't bitch. Fix!
But, remember that you can't change what
you first don't acknowledge!"
Casandra

TRUISM: "To resent is to re-infect." Casandra

AMAZING ADVENTURE #27

A 'ROCK' FROM THE 'ROCK'!

2003.
This is a true story.

"What do you think?" my friend gushed as she waved her hand under my nose. There, on the third finger of her left hand, twinkled a diamond ring – a real 'rock' we would say.

"Wow!" I answered. "Does this mean you are getting married?" I asked rather shocked.

This new man was more than ten years younger than my newly widowed friend, and they had only been dating a few months. I had known how lonely she had been since her husband death and I also knew she really wanted to have a man in her life again. 'The love of her life,' as she often proclaimed him, was now gone but I think in her heart of hearts she was desperate to recapture that feeling once again.

Having met her new man only a few times, I hugged her and wished her well, keeping my reservations to myself. He was in his late forties, she in her early sixties. He had never married. This would be her third. He had lived at home with his parents until recently moving from Newfoundland. He was employed, but was extremely frugal, or as some might say – cheap - preferring to spend her ample resources. He owned no property; she was a substantial land owner. I'm sure you don't have to be psychic to know what I was thinking!

Nevertheless, I said nothing until the phone rang one day several months before the proposed wedding. It was to be a lavish affair in Newfoundland, hosted by his parents and I was to be the mistress of ceremonies. We had been happily discussing wedding details and catching up as she now lived quite a distance from me, when she asked, "Casandra, will you do a reading for me?"

"Sure. What do you want to know?"

We had developed a system whereby she would ask her questions. I would get off the phone and go into my meditative state, calling her back with what I got.

"I'd just like you to do a reading on my new man, that's all." She knew enough to say very little.

Later that evening, I did just that. I focused on his name and he soon came into my mind. I 'saw' some disturbing details about his youth, but that is another story. What came through in full force was, "there will be no wedding - life long friends perhaps - but no marriage!"

"What do I do with this?" I thought. I picked up the phone to tell her.

Perhaps, we are not meant to know things ahead of time. Life reveals itself through its very processes, for she listened to my answer and replied, "Oh, I think you've got it wrong this time, Casandra. Everything is fine between us."

I've learned not to take it personally when I appear to be wrong for I have been wrong on occasion. That's the fun of it all! Life keeps us guessing!

The plans for the wedding went ahead. My flight to Newfoundland or 'the Rock' as we Canadians affectionately call this bald, barren promontory sticking out into the Atlantic Ocean, was uneventful. That is until I arrived.

I was scarcely out of the taxi when she met me in the driveway. Taking me by the arm, she breathlessly whispered in my ear.

"We've got a problem! He won't sign the prenup!"

I may have neglected to mention that her oldest son was an estate lawyer, very protective of his mother's assets and was bearing down on her prospective husband at this very moment to sign or else!

It was not going well. The groom was intractable. The wedding was the next day with half of Newfoundland invited. It turned out his family was quite well connected and were very much anticipating that this marriage would add to their asset base.

"What am I going to do?" she wailed. Then in the next breath she told me!

We are going forward with a 'dummy' ceremony she said. There will be no marriage document signed. It won't be a legal wedding, but it will save all this embarrassment until I can figure out what I want to do!

"Are you okay with this? Will you still be the mistress of ceremonies?"

What are friends for? I did as I was asked. She looked beautiful in her gown. We then packed and left town!

She kept the 'rock' from the 'rock' but there was no marriage. I guess I was wrong about one thing, though. They did not remain life long friends but, I do remember a 'perhaps' with that statement!

TRUISM: "There is light at the end of every tunnel and it's not always that of a freight train!" Casandra

AMAZING ADVENTURE #28

FRED IN THE CLOSET

2004.
This is a true story.

"Where are you?" I called upstairs to my granddaughter.

"I'm playing in my room." she answered. "Come see."

Almost two now, busy and precocious, she was a bright, happy, curly headed delight!

I stood in the doorway of her room and looked over her domain. Large and spacious, it appeared to me to have everything a little girl could want. Everywhere there was whimsy and fantasy. From the poufy printed quilt and fluffy pillows covering her bed to a squat, legless overstuffed, brightly coloured chair plumped in the corner, easier for her little legs to climb up on, to angels and cherubs looking lovingly down from their wall sconces, with stuffed unicorns and teddies peeking out from every corner, to the canopy of sheer gauze draped over her bed, it could have been right out of a fairy tale! The room also had a private reading nook built into one wall! Three feet up from the floor and about the size of a large closet, it too contained a bed stuffed with plump pillows, a small stool positioned so that she could climb in and curl up with her books in cozy confinement. Last of all was the large walk in closet, big enough to play house in, filled with all manner of dress-up clothes and toys where she would often declare she was busy playing with "Fred"!

We had become accustomed to her references to Fred. Imaginary childhood playmates had been common to many of us in the family so we respectfully acknowledged his importance.

"Fred lives in the closet," she would answer when queried about him. "He comes to play with me."

It did strike as a little strange that her imaginary playmate had the rather unusual name, 'Fred'. It was not a common name at this time and no one that we knew was called Fred. At least no one now alive! Her great grandmother had had a brother named Fred who had been tragically struck and killed by a train when he was returning from visiting his girlfriend to whom he had just proposed. Even though the story was common family folklore, it had never been discussed in front of children for it would have been inappropriate. The choice of name also gave us pause, because my father, her grandfather, had had the middle name, Frederick. We did wonder, as was our belief, if someone whom we had known and loved, now 'on the other side', was about to return to us.

And so it was that, 'Fred in the Closet' came up in conversations fairly frequently as we would often ask after him.

On this particular afternoon, I was staying at my daughter's home. She had just given birth to a son, a first grandson for me, and I was there helping out.

As I stood in the doorway, watching my granddaughter busily arranging her toys, I thought to ask her. "Were you playing with Fred?"

"Oh no, Grandma, Fred's here now."

I looked around. "You mean he's in the room with us now?" I asked.

"No. No. He's **here** now." She looked up at me as if to say, "Don't you get it?"

She never mentioned Fred in the closet again. She didn't need to. Fred was in the crib now.

TRUISM: "Your life is your gift to unwrap. Don't be opening others' 'present'!" Casandra

AMAZING ADVENTURE #29
IS IT A LITTLE BOY?

2004.
This is a true story.

"Is it a little boy?" I asked straining to see from behind the masked and gowned doctor. My oldest daughter was at that very moment in full labour with her second child. Lucky enough to be able to once again witness the birth of a grandchild and sincerely wishing only that the child be healthy, a small part of me still very much wanted to know its sex. Was my prediction to be proven right? Was this the much awaited and envisioned grandson with whom I had imagined walking Florida beaches? At that time I had neither a Florida residence nor a grandson. Now with a home there, I wondered, was the second part to come to pass? Months before, the ultra sound had shown a very large baby with an exceptionally big hand which appeared to be waving at us! The technician had said she was ninety per cent sure it was a boy. Life is full of surprises I well knew and technology, sometimes just like psychics, was proved to be inaccurate!

Thus the anxious question, "Is it a little boy?"

"No," came the short reply from the busy family doctor. He did rather have his hands full I thought as I reflected on his terseness.

He was beloved by my daughter as well as by most of this small northern town. Even though I had only met him briefly on occasion,

I'm sure he knew of my desire to have a grandson - almost everyone did - and I knew of his love of a good joke!

"Is it a little girl?" I asked again, somewhat disappointed.

Again came the same reply, "No."

As we were all wondering just what alien life form was about to present itself, he chuckled and finished his sentence.

"He's not little!" he quipped, laughing gleefully as he helped a plump, rosy baby boy with a final push from his mother enter this world. He then placed him lovingly across my daughter's abdomen.

Tears, hugs and squeals of delight filled the delivery room as he whispered into her ear, "You'll be fine this time, dear. We won't let anything happen."

Later, from others, we were to hear how he had mentally rehearsed all possible delivery outcomes planning his strategy so that she would avoid the complications which had almost taken her life once before.

"Ten pounds, one ounce!" the nurse announced after she had weighed my new grandson. "Well, that part of my prediction came true," I thought to myself. "Should I let them know what else I 'see' I mused?

Why there had been any question in my mind as to his arrival I cannot explain except to say that even with many, many proven predictions, I can still doubt. My study of psychics throughout history- a subject of endless fascination for me – even to the discovery of the meaning of my name – but that is another story – has shown me even gifted viewers of future events are sometimes given just a tantalizing glimpse of what is to be. Often, there is a 'twist' and things do not come about exactly as perceived - almost as if there would be no fun in knowing everything. Life can be just like a gift— wrapped and anticipated. We psychics may help to 'shake the package', but each event is yours and only yours to open and never before its time!

Several months before his birth, I had 'gone to visit' my grandson by connecting with his energy while he was still sheltered and protected within his mother's womb.

"I'm psychic just like you, Grandma," had come his small voice. His energy was quiet and solid, calm, as if there was no rush for absolutely anything. That was all he had said, but then knowledge of his future had streamed through my consciousness.

A strong male voice 'spoke'. "He will build on your foundation. He is a healer and has come to this planet to mend the schism between male and female energies. He will present as a male, large of body and very strong, but will have a very well developed empathy for all females. His psychic abilities will far surpass yours. A great speaker, he will draw great crowds to hear his message of healing."

And there it had been. I have written it here as a record for him should he ever be interested.

Only six years of age at this writing, he is large of body and has had some challenges with his physical development. The ligaments connecting muscle to bone are underdeveloped which causes all physical activity to require more energy than normal. Consequently he tires easily, but my daughter had his condition diagnosed early and has been told if he is kept active, at puberty it will self correct. He is a great lover of books and is well above grade level in reading. But is he psychic you ask?

There is only one instance I am aware of. Seated at the kitchen table one afternoon when he was nearing three years of age, he informed his mother he was sad. When queried he said something bad had just happened and lots of people were crying.

He didn't seem upset himself but simply reported what he knew.

It was later we heard an automobile crash on the trans-Canada highway a few miles away had occurred about the time of his statement. Several people had been killed and there was indeed great sadness.

Did he 'see' it?

For now we leave the issue of his psychic ability undiscussed. If it is so, it is his gift and his alone to unwrap.

TRUISM: "Every time I close the door on reality, it comes through the windows!" Casandra

AMAZING ADVENTURE #30
THE DRAGONFLY DAY

2005.
This is a true story.

On my own now for well over a year, despondent, but determined not to make the same mistake again, I had cut men from my life. No dating, nothing. I focused instead on healing from the break up of my second relationship.

My grandson had been born six weeks after I had separated. I was numb. I could feel no joy in this much awaited arrival. A zombie going through the motions, I spent time at my daughter's trying to be of help, but just hanging on. A sense of failure and deep hopelessness settled over me. You might say I was throwing a real pity party and I was the only guest. For over a year now I had been indulging in self-inflicted suffering and sabotage. Those may appear to be harsh words of condemnation, but when I look back upon that time, I realize the pain I felt was because of the way I had chosen to perceive what had happened.

Had my prayer to be 'done' not been answered? And speedily as well, but that is another story!

Alone now in my beautifully decorated high-rise condo, my bills were paid, my income secure and I was travelling the world. So much so, that I was the envy of all my married girlfriends. They called me the 'jet setter' as I was off to Paris, New York city, Las Vegas and more!

Was I running - probably? It seemed if I stopped doing, I might stop being.

The early morning sun warmed my face; I cupped the mug of tea in my hands and slid down into the deck chair. My daughter's large backyard was fringed with tall, stately pines, private and sheltered. It was quiet this time of day, yet to be filled with the chatter of my grandchildren as they romped over the deck with their golden retriever or bounced on their trampoline. My eyes surveyed my daughter's domain - the grass needed cutting and paint was peeling from the deck furniture, both of which would have caused her to sigh with some unhappiness, for she loved beauty and order. It was a lot to keep this household humming and she did almost everything herself. My son-in-law was not a handy man, preferring to spend his free time on the hockey rink as coach and player, leaving the home for her to maintain. Consequently, it may not have been a perfectly ordered household, but it held a lot of love. It was a home where children painted the inside of the kitchen cupboards with their handprints, butterflies and dragons. Where the dress up box was never far away, and beds were piled with story books and stuffed animal friends! Plays were performed, music and laughter were in the air - quite honestly, it was exhilarating yet exhausting to be there!

If I could not be happy here.....?

"How long is this pain to last?! Will I always be alone?!" I wailed internally, oblivious to the happiness around me.

The dragonfly landed on my hand. Large and luminous it was bigger than most. It sat, folding and unfolding its wings. Startled by its arrival, I waited, still, wondering how long it planned to stay. Time ticked by and still it stayed, its wings keeping time with the beating of my heart. My breathing slowed down, my thinking slowed down. This beautiful creature became my focus. Drawn in by its iridescent colours catching the rays of the morning sun, the purples, blues and gold bouncing from its luminous beating wings, I was drawn out of myself. Here was something truly beautiful and it had chosen me!

My head turned at the sound of the patio door opening.

My daughter was stepping out onto the deck.

"Come see…" I started to say just as the beautiful creature took flight.

"Oh, you just missed a gorgeous dragonfly!" I exclaimed. "It sat on my hand for the longest time."

"You know what they say about them, don't you? They're angels come to give you a message!" she said with a smile and a good morning hug.

That evening there was to be a gathering of my daughter's spiritual group. They met every week, but this particular night was special as it was a social evening held at a friend's cottage and I had been invited.

A beautiful lakeside setting, a large, spacious porch overlooking the water came complete with a rocking chair! What could make me happier I thought as I headed directly for it? I had sat there most of the night, enjoying the conversation and beautiful setting, and only when I stood to leave, did I notice what was on the wall behind my head. I stared in disbelief. Tears pricked at the corner of my eyes.

"Are you alright?" my hostess asked. She must have seen the colour drain from my face.

"That plaque on the wall above my head…." I stammered.

"Oh that." she said. "My father made it. He always said they were angels bringing messages!" she chuckled.

I stared once again at the image of TWO beautifully carved dragonflies flying in tandem with the words etched underneath, "HEARTS CONTENT"!

"My last name's Hart," was all I could mumble.

TRUISM: "I have only one rule and it's golden." Casandra

AMAZING ADVENTURE #31

THE CHRISTMAS BELL

2005.
This is a true story.

(What follows is an excerpt from a journal written January 1st. 2006)

Today I began to write in this lovely journal my oldest daughter gave to me for Christmas. May it grow to contain thoughts, memories and glimpses into my life that may cause others one day to marvel. For my life appears to me to be a miracle –small coincidences and fortuitous happenings seem to unfold daily now. There is no doubt in my mind that an unseen force guides and directs all that occurs here on this spinning space ship called earth!

Let me share with you just one such 'small happening'.

For years as a grade school teacher, I loved to share the picture story book by Chris VanAllsburg called, 'The Polar Express'. From the moment I first read it I felt inspired to share it every Christmas with all the children I taught and loved. So it was that that my granddaughter received a copy for her first Christmas. Inside the cover I had written the words, 'May we always hear the bell'.

For if you know the story, you understand the phrase to be a metaphor for keeping 'the child within' forever present in your life. To hear the bell is to believe in a creative force greater than oneself; to believe in the magic nature of being and to accept that miracles can occur every day!

On this particular Christmas Eve, my daughter's small family and I had just returned from a 'magical' children's pageant at the local church, and were preparing to tuck a sleepy, curly headed three year old in with the required bedtime story.

She had been urging her father to drive quickly over the icy northern town roads for she had heard over the car radio that Santa was on his way, his sleigh somewhere in the very vicinity of her house!

Cookies and milk had been placed on Santa's own special plate and cup, stockings had been hung, and all was quiet throughout the house as I now opened the book to read. I began with the inscription on the blank fly leaf – the very one I had alluded to earlier in this story. As I did, my daughter and I exchanged knowing glances which said, "Yes, belief in the magic of life is so important!"

As all three of us snuggled together in the soft sofa, I handed the book to my daughter and she began to read. The house still and peaceful, a feeling of contentment filled us as we turned the beautifully illustrated pages and read the story once again.

A few pages along, mid-sentence, she stopped reading.

"Did you hear that?" my daughter asked, a look of wonder spreading across her face!

I knew exactly what she was referring to for I had heard it as well - a sound, faint, as if off in the distance, but unmistakable! It was not of this world, I knew, and yet somehow it was so real, so present. I had heard what I heard.

That unmistakable jingle of metal tinkling against metal – such a joyous sound – so distinctive – a sound any northerner who has ever had the privilege of being pulled over icy hills and dales in a horse drawn sleigh would know instantly! Yes, it could have only been the sound of sleigh bells!

As my daughter and I stared incredulously into each other's eyes, our mouths both formed the word, "Bells?"

In that instant, my granddaughter jumped from the sofa with the words, "Santa!" on her little lips as she bolted for the stairs.

"Santa's here! I heard him, Mommy. He's here!"

With that, roaring with laughter and filled with glee my daughter and I followed her little slippered feet up the stairs to her bed.

Oh what fun it was! Had she heard the sound too? How delightful and what a Christmas memory this was to make, I thought to myself.

By the time we reached her door, she was already tucked into bed. Eyes closed tightly for she had to appear asleep for Santa was here!

We kissed her face and tiptoed back down the stairs, bursting to say. "Did you really hear them?! What could it have been? There's no one here but us. Who could have made the sound?"

These were the questions that tumbled out of us several times over as we attempted to find a rational explanation, and then, as so often you must with all miracles, we shrugged our shoulders and accepted with wonder the unexplainable.

A sign - for those of us who believe – absolutely! For those who do not – just an unexplained occurrence with a logical explanation - somewhere.

As for me, now in the sixth decade of my life, it is pure joy to have heard the bell! My wish is that I continue to do so until I decide to leave this earth.

Blessing to all and in your homes may you, 'live, laugh and talk much' as the plague on my daughter's kitchen wall suggests and may your child within 'always hear the bell'!

TRUISM: APPLES & WINE

Women are like apples on trees.
The best ones are at the top of the tree.
Most men don't want to reach for the good ones
Because they are afraid of falling and getting hurt.
Instead, they sometimes take the apples from the ground
That aren't as good, but easy.
The apples at the top think something is wrong
with them, when in reality, they're amazing.
They just have to wait for the right man to come along,
The one who's brave enough to climb all
the way to the top of the tree.

Now men…..
Men are like wine.
They begin as grapes,
And it's up to women to stomp the *@#* out of them,
Until they turn into something acceptable to have dinner with!
Anonymous

AMAZING ADVENTURE #32

A BURNED OUT BASEMENT OF A HEART

2006.
This is a true story.

I may be psychic, but that doesn't mean I'm smart! At least when it has come to my love life, my errors in judgment have never been revealed to me ahead of time. It was as if I were meant to learn from hindsight rather than foresight!

I was single again! My thirteen year relationship with my companion and mentor had come crashing to an end. In a matter of hours the man who had supported the development of my psychic abilities through facilitating hundreds of readings in the board room of his real estate office, was gone from my life. But that is another story!

Months later, staring at a passenger list for a singles' cruise I had just booked, I saw a name and the thought flashed through my mind, "You will be in my life!" I 'knew' this man would be important to me, but here is where psychic insights can be challenging. For good or ill was not revealed.

My mind raced ahead to thoughts of, 'he's the one!' Already an obsession was beginning to form around my 'recognition' of his name. Having guided hundreds of women suffering from debilitating fixations on all the 'wrong' men in their lives, one would think I would recognize the symptoms.

No, I packed my bags for the cruise with all my most alluring outfits, convinced I would soon be part of a happy couple once again! My 'lonely days and lonely nights' were soon to be behind me I thought!

A veteran of many cruises and a very successful businessman, he was considered quite a catch. Unfortunately, he thought so too and had married twice, uncommitted to either relationship. He was fond of dating women much younger than he and did it well and often!

In fact, on this cruise he had spent his time with a young, fit armed forces captain and was planning to fly north to escort her to a high ranking military ball after this trip. The end of the week was fast approaching and he had consequently been MIA at all the mixers so I had written off my psychic insight until my roommate, a reporter for the San Diego Times, told me she was on assignment and writing an article on singles' cruising. She was going to interview him that afternoon because he had been on so many of these cruises!

What part of, "this guy has all the signs of being a PLAYER," did I not recognize?"

"Can I come?" It was out of my mouth before my brain was in gear and off we went!

As soon as I laid eyes on him, I was done like dinner! Now, you might ask, how could you like someone you don't even know yet? That is a very sensible question, but when an obsession hits, all logic is out the window. Rarely am I at a loss for words except when I really like a man. So there I sat, hanging on his every word and anyone who would care to could see, I had an enormous crush!

He now started showing up at the mixers and even stopped by to chat with me. We exchanged email addresses and he said he would keep in touch, which he did-from his next cruise – a month long tour of Scandinavia. As I eagerly read accounts of his adventures, I ignored the fact that there was never the mention of a companion. He was travelling alone? I knew what a single ticket would cost, but nevertheless, intelligent questions such as, "Are you with anyone? Are you in a relationship now?" just would not write themselves into my email correspondence. No, I was just too busy 'selling' myself to look at whether or not I should be.

Months and months passed. Eagerly awaited emails came sporadically from him. I became more and more obsessed. It was like playing chess. What should I reveal? What should I not reveal? How could I convince him I was the 'girl of his dreams'? Was he just playing hard to get or was he proceeding cautiously, afraid of rejection, unsure of himself where I was concerned, because I was such a self-proclaimed catch!!!

He was going to be in Las Vegas he had informed me so I decided some gambling might be in order. My mother informed me this was a bad idea.

"You're chasing him! A man should come to you! This will not go well!"

Did I mention that I had inherited the psychic gene from her?!

I dismissed her views as old fashioned and I packed. I would stay in my favourite hotel, but he would pick me up at the airport and 'show me the town'!

Tossing and turning in my bed the night before my departure, tears of self pity once again flowed. "How was it that I was single again?" I cried. I ached for a man! What an emotional mess I was! Curled up in the fetal position on my bed, sobbing in the darkened room, suddenly a stream of brilliant sparkling lights raced past my closed eye lids and a whooshing sound of air rushed by my ears. I have experienced this several times and I can only describe it like being catapulted into a Star Wars like warp drive!

"He will bring you great pain," came a voice in the darkness. "He will take you to the very depths of yourself!"

A vision of fiery orange flames licking at my body caused me to clutch my stomach, folding in on myself. I cried out with pain it hurt so.

The vision spent; there came a room filling stillness. I knew what I had heard to be true, but I also knew it could not be avoided. There was a lesson here. Accepting that knowledge, I hugged my knees to my chest and rocking back and forth to comfort myself, fell into a deep sleep.

He was indeed at the airport. The perfect gentleman, he showed me the town including his home before taking me to my hotel. It was as if he were laying out before me all that he had to offer. As we surveyed his back yard complete with sand bottomed pool, hot tub and tiki bar the thought went through my head – this is a real swinging bachelor pad. It was as if he read my mind. Slipping his arm around my waist, he leaned into me and whispered into my ear, "This could all be given up if the right girl came along."

Hook, line and sinker - he reeled me in! I was his! Insane, I know, but I already had visions of redecorating his home and making it mine!

To make a long story short or just to make another short story, I will leave the details of our love affair for another story!

You probably don't need to be psychic to know how it all ended.

Once again, I had flown to be with him. Once again, I suspected there were other women in his life, but never found the courage to confront or ask him if there was a future for us. I settled for crumbs, I am ashamed to say. Even his best friend had taken me aside and told me, "You're too good for him."

Sitting up in the bed sobbing, I was in deep, emotional self-inflicted pain. Because we had just finished making love, which he had declared incredibly intoxicating, he was confused. Tenderly he put his hand on my back as he propped himself up on one arm to ask, "What is it? What's wrong?"

How could I tell him I wanted so badly to hear a declaration of his love, his reassurance that he would spend the rest of his life loving me, when I couldn't even ask when he would see me next? Insanely obsessed with him, making love was like visiting another realm. He was my drug of choice. I was addicted. Oh, how powerfully intoxicating can be the feelings of unrequited love - such exquisite suffering!

"I don't know why you are in my life." I wailed. "What's the reason?" I wanted to add, 'for all this suffering', but I dared not reveal the depth of my feeling.

Quietly, he said, "Perhaps it is you who are in my life for a reason."

With that I collapsed into his arms, my hand falling upon his heart and once again, there was a whoosh of sound over my ears and I 'saw' into him. It was as if, for that briefest of moments, I was looking down at his exposed heart. It laid, in a deep crater surrounded by a barren landscape, a tangled mass of smoldering, blackened ashes. Like a bombed out basement, the dwelling above it, and all life around, obliterated, annihilated!

"This is who he is now," came the words, "for fear of the pain of ever loving again, he has killed his soul. He is lost to you."

Filled with new understanding and compassion, I curled tighter into him. I said quietly, "I love you."

There was no reply.

I had expected none and it mattered not. I was going to be fine. Realizing the greatest love of all was the love of self, the spell was broken. I was back. I could now take my leave of this man for my love could not bring him back to himself.

He alone could find the way.

TRUISM: "Follow the bread crumbs. They will lead you 'home'. The universe is always leaving tell tale signs!" Casandra

AMAZING ADVENTURE #33

DOUBTING THOMAS

2007.
This is a true story.

"Is this Reverend Hart?" a worried woman's voice asked as I picked up the phone.

"Yes," I answered.

"Well, I have a problem I hope you can help me with." She sped on, "I'm here at the Highland Funeral Home and we have a situation. We have been asked to do the service for a Mr. Ray Thomas and because he was an agnostic, none of the pastors we usually call on will do it. Would you?" she finally took a breath.

Learning the hard way to 'judge not, lest ye be judged,' I answered, "I'd be happy to."

I worked hard on his service. It was a challenge to comfort loved ones without reference to God or an afterlife, but using a passage which compared life to a train journey, his family agreed, would be acceptable to Ray.

And so I began.

I imagine life can be like a train ride. We get on. We ride. We get off. There are accidents and there are delays. At certain stops there are surprises - some will translate into great moments of joy; some will result in profound sorrow. Some people consider their journey like a happy tour. They will just go merrily along. Others will encounter many upsets, fears, and losses on their journeys. Others still, will offer a helping hand to others in need. Ray was one of those.

He constantly strove to understand his travel companions and look for the best in everyone for he understood the bigger mystery of our journey is that we don't know when our last stop will come. Sadly, his has.

Before turning the service over to the many individuals who came forward to pay tribute to a beloved man, I then read the words of a poem, which I had adapted to reflect Ray's final wish.

> For this is a journey we all must take,
> And each must go alone.
> It's all a part of a master plan,
> A step on the road to final rest..

"Miss Me But Let Me Go" by Betty Miller Davis

Sad silence filled the packed room as we filed out, a testament to this deeply loved man and the fact that his departure at the age of fifty seven was a great loss. Pews had been filled to overflowing with family, friends, coworkers and students for he had been a man who had taught, worked and volunteered extensively in his community. His journey had indeed been one of looking for the best in everyone, including himself. Throughout a productive life, however, he had remained steadfast in his rejection of a 'higher power' or force in the universe greater than himself. Convinced it would simply be, 'ashes to ashes, dust to dust' at the end of his days, his instruction to have no religious references at his service had been very clear.

In spite of this, overwhelmed and uplifted by the outpouring of love and praise of this man's life, as I left the building, I couldn't help myself. I raised my eyes to the open blue spring sky and gave thanks to God. I gave thanks for bringing me this opportunity to serve and I gave thanks especially to Ray for allowing me to give his goodbye.

"I just know you are up there now, Ray, having a great time surrounded by loved ones who came to greet you."

I laughed as I spoke these words out loud to the empty sky, not really caring who heard me or what they would think.

"I guess you know now, that another ride on the train awaits you!"

A smile filled me at the thought of Ray's surprise at discovering this end was just another beginning!

I pulled out of the parking lot onto the busy street, a large truck in front of me blocking my view.

"I wish he would change lanes so I can see what's ahead of me," I mused. In spite of my deep belief that I am always guided and protected by a loving Lord, I often fall into the error thinking that I'm all there is and have to make my own way - and quickly!

No sooner had I the thought than the truck changed lanes, leaving me a clear view of the back of a bus!

But then, I stared in disbelief at what had been revealed. Never have I seen this before or since. I am sure Ray would have used a train if one had been available.

What the sign was advertising, I do not know. All I saw were the bold red letters of an advertisement splashed across a white background which read simply,

"RAY KNOWS".

TRUISM: "Love deeply and passionately. You may get hurt but, not by regret." Casandra

AMAZING ADVENTURE #34

LOVERS AND FRIENDS

2007.
This is a true story.

"Oh my God, he's really here!" I rolled over in my friend's big guest room bed and covered my head with a pillow. I could hear the muffled rumble of the Harley's engine and I groaned. Why had I had so much red wine last night I wondered? I had been drinking quite a lot of the stuff lately.

"Drowning my sorrows," I mumbled as I got out of bed and started pulling on my clothes. My head ached. Hangovers were becoming far too frequent. My body was speaking out loud and clear, but was I listening?!

"Good morning!" My friend greeted me with a sly look. "He's here to take you to breakfast just like he said he would!"

"Hmmmmmm," was what I managed. Did I really say I would love a ride on that thing? What was I thinking?!"

And there he was standing in the doorway with a smile that lit up the room! He was a big man, both in size and energy. His rich baritone voice rumbled, "Ready?"

I had first met him about ten years before. Newly separated, he had been renting a room at my friend's bed and breakfast and when he heard a psychic was coming to visit he was curious enough to want a reading. I had agreed to do it.

As soon as he spoke, I knew he had been born in Europe. He was Dutch and had come to this country at the age of twelve.

Obviously devastated by the breakup of his twenty six year marriage, he was seeking answers. There was an, 'aha moment', when it was realized, that rather than give his wife every material thing, it was the gift of himself she had most wanted.

I had gone on to predict he would return to Holland and there meet a woman and fall in love. (I was wrong, but that is this story!)

Now single, I was once again coming to give readings and my friend had asked if he might be interested in being my dinner companion. He had asked, in typical single man fashion, "Does she still look the same?"(He tells me now that the ten years had been kind to me.)

And that is how I came to drink too much wine, wake up with a hangover with a promised ride on the big Harley parked now in my friend's driveway.

Dinner the night before had been fun and lively, but even though I had enjoyed his company there had been no 'thunder bolt' moment – no thought of 'is there a future here?'

Perhaps it was because he appeared a little rough around the edges. A 'tool belt' kind of guy, I was more used to the CEO types. In his plaid shirt and blue jeans, with big rough, work worn hands, he was definitely a change of pace for me.

"Why had I agreed to do this?" was all I could think as I nervously fumbled with the helmet. Smiling down at me, he helped me fasten it securely under my chin.

We stood shoulder to shoulder next to his motorcycle, him giving me some tips as to what to expect, me trying not to tremble in the early morning spring air.

"Hop on" he said and I did.

Well…. not really - it was more like grabbing hold of my own leg and pulling it up and over and then, when my bottom hit the seat, wrapping my arms tightly around his waist, holding on as if my life depended upon it, as the big blue machine rumbled, roared and vibrated under us.

He was good, very good. Having ridden a motorcycle for more than twenty years, he knew how to handle a bike, and as it turned out, me as well! Deftly, he maneuvered us down the long lane and out onto the highway. Each time he shifted gears, the bike roared, I hung on tighter and he laughed louder obviously enjoying an experience that never failed to thrill him!

He took great care to take great care of me! Gradually I relaxed into the experience - the sights and smells of the open road and the sensation of raw power between my legs - which with him so masterfully in charge seemed safely exciting.

He stopped often, each time helping with my helmet and asking if I wanted more. What had started out as a short breakfast run turned into a day long date. At dusk, back at the B&B, he asked if he could kiss me goodnight. A brief brush of my cheek with his lips and the 'Harley Man', as I had started to think of him, was gone.

Summer came and went. I was keeping busy. Whenever my friend asked if her friend had called, my standard response was, "He's just not that into me or he would have called by now. Let's forget it."

To be honest, my heart was a bombed out basement at this point - obliterated, incapable of feeling. I gave the lack of attention from my 'Harley man' little thought, my mind filled with an unhealthy obsession! Deep in a life lesson, I was 'nailing myself to the cross' once again. You think I would know better. I was teaching workshops on relationships! What is that saying, "We teach what we most need to learn?!" Didn't I often quote Dolly Parton herself when I was once again counseling a woman who had lost all her dignity over a man, telling her – "Get down off the cross, honey. We need the wood!"

Whether or not he called was not an issue. It was not for his call I cried by the phone.

No, the object of my obsession was a man my friends derogatorily referred to as my, 'Vegas Venture'.

Was it because he had a home in Las Vegas or because they believed this was one gamble I was sure to lose?

But that is another story!

Meanwhile, spring had now turned into fall, when my 'Harley man' finally called. He was in town and would I like to meet him for coffee he asked? He lived over two hours from me, but often had business in the city, so it did not seem too unusual.

Distracted, unhappy, obsessing over another man, I said what any dysfunctional woman would.

I said, "Sure."

Across the restaurant table, he smiled at me. If he was nervous, I didn't notice as I wasn't noticing too much these days other than my own self inflicted suffering. I was throwing the equivalent of a spiritual temper tantrum because I was not getting the man I thought I wanted! Here was a great guy sitting right in front of me and I could not see! Sound familiar anyone?

Instead, I reached across the table for his hand, looked into his incredibly blue eyes and said, "I don't really see any potential here for a long term relationship, but if you just want to be lovers and friends that works for me."

Wow! Had I just said that? I waited for his reaction.

"I'll take what I can get," he said calmly and just kept on smiling with those big, blue eyes focused right on my face.

Later, after many months of dating when I asked why he would settle for those terms, he calmly stated, "I knew if I hung around long enough, you'd fall in love with me!"

You've gotta love that kind of confidence and I do! It's now almost five years since that first ride and we have set a date to be married!

Now, you may wonder why I've included this story in my psychic adventures! Well, let me tell you!

Psychics go to psychics too. Did you know that? It is very rare that we can read for ourselves. So in 1989 I had been introduced to a wonderful, eccentric little woman who lived in a tiny house with furniture covered in plastic and five locks on her door, but who turned out to be the most incredible psychic I have ever experienced!

Sloshing tea around in a china cup to read the leaves, and then laying out ordinary playing cards in rows in front of her, she would predict events with uncanny accuracy. I have written records of her predictions that go back now over twenty years with almost all having come to pass.

At the time of this first reading I had been unhappily married for almost twenty-one years and believed I was doomed to never escape. In mid sentence, this tiny wrinkled woman had looked me directly in the face and asked, 'Has anyone ever told you that you will be married three times?"

"Good God, I thought! How is that possible? I can't even imagine getting out of the first one!"

She then went on to predict many details about my second husband including the colour of his hair, his business and the initial of his last name! My third husband she said less about.

"He will be a foreigner. He will marry you if **you** want marriage."

Sixteen years later, single again after my second marriage, I take a ride on a motorcycle with a man born and raised in Holland who speaks fluent Dutch. I believe that would fulfill her prediction of a 'foreigner'.

Two years later we move in together and two years after that **I** propose! He was waiting for me to ask!

How is it that a tiny little woman looking at tea leaves and playing cards could 'see' thirty years into my future, you ask?

Is the knowledge of our future held within each of us – a gift to be discovered? Do psychics help us to ignore the, 'no peeking!' sticker on the package?

What fun it is to unwrap our 'present'!

TRUISM: "Love is the ability and willingness to allow those you care for to be what they choose for themselves without any insistence that they satisfy you." Wayne Dyer

AMAZING ADVENTURE #35

YOUR FUTURE IS IN YOUR HANDS!

2007.
This is a true story.

He looked past me as we sipped our morning tea at the breakfast café. Clifton Hill, the main street in Niagara Falls, was not that busy with tourists as yet and we were enjoying our weekend getaway. I turned to see what he was looking at.

"Let's go and get it done," he said.

"You've got to be kidding! I didn't think you believed in all that stuff!" was my response.

"C'mom. It'll be fun." He said as I stared at the sign which read: 'Psalmest. Fortunes Read Here.'

We paid our bill and ran across the street, laughing, holding hands.

Maybe it would be fun I thought, but a memory of a time when it hadn't been flicked through my mind.

Several summers before, while still in a relationship with the second man in my life, strolling along the main street of our town, browsing, enjoying my time off from teaching, I had seen a very similar sign in a storefront window. A woman just inside the door was seated at a small table, and she beckoned me to enter.

Being psychic myself, I rarely felt the need to seek the insights of others, but this day, I felt compelled to walk through her doorway.

Seated across from her, I stretched out my right hand. She turned it over gently, cupped it in hers, dark haired and dark of face, her brow now furrowed in concentration. The room around us was dimly lit, the smell of a newly extinguished cigarette hung in the air and I remembered thinking, "This is one that gives the rest of us a bad name."

I have since learned that divine intelligence uses all manner of means to express itself and perhaps by my judgment of others I only succeed in giving myself a bad name!

With a throaty rumble she cleared her voice and said simply, flatly, "Unlucky in love."

"What??" I stammered. "What do you mean?"

"See this?" she asked as she traced her finger over a crease in my palm.

"That's your love line and it tells me that you will have no luck in love."

"But, I'm in a great relationship with a wonderful man now and have been for over a dozen years! You must be wrong!"

"All I can tell is what I see," she responded and went on to give me more information, none of which I can record here for I truly heard none of it, my shock at her opening statement being so great.

"That'll be ten dollars," was what I heard next and with that I rallied enough to fish a bill out of my wallet and exit her storefront.

"Well, that was a total waste of time and money," I thought to myself as I headed home to the condo I shared with the second man in my life.

Less than a year later, that very same man shattered my world, but that is another story!

The Clifton Hill storefront was filled with light as we entered. A bell over the door announced our arrival. The psychic asked which of us would like to be first and then took us in turn into a smaller room for our reading. Much of what she told me seemed to fit, but it was only when, after our individual readings, as we sat chatting with her together, that she looked directly at us and said, "Soul mates. You two are soul mates- meant to be together. You are very compatible -deep love here."

I squirmed a bit in the chair. We had been seeing each other now for almost two years, but only on a casual basis. In my mind, I was still looking for that 'perfect mate' and had not yet recognized he was right in front of me.

A patient man, he was not nearly as perturbed by her prediction as I. Much later, engaged to be married, I had asked him how it was that he had been able to wait so long for me to figure it out.

He simply said, "I knew that if I hung around long enough, you would fall in love with me."

You have to love that kind of confidence in a man!

We are happily married now and I do truly believe we are soul mates. He is the third man in my life and was accurately predicted and described by a psychic more than thirty years before we met, but that is also another story!

How is it that such simple things as cards, tea leaves or crystal balls often reveal our future, or that even something as mundane as the simple lines and creases of our palm can be a road map of our life?

So you see, your future can truly be in your hands - literally and figuratively.

TRUISM: "A tragedy can turn out to be our greatest good if we approach it in ways from which we can grow." Louise Hay

AMAZING ADVENTURE #36

DEATH AT MY DOOR AGAIN?

2007-2013
This is a true story.

"It's back. Oh, sweet Jesus, Casandra. Tell me it's not back again!' You know how I hate that fucking cancer!"

Fear filled the otherwise jovial face of my new neighbour and friend as I put my hand gently on her shoulder.

"You'll be fine. It's nothing. The tests will show it's nothing."

There had been a time when the tests had been something, and that is this story.

It was December 2007 and there were new people to meet and new places to see on the arm of the man I would eventually marry, but that is also another story.

Anxious to introduce his new lady to his friends, two weeks before Christmas he ushered me into a friend's living room in his home town, handed me a festive drink and proceeded to tell my new acquaintances I was psychic!

I squirmed in my seat, glanced nervously at the couple who had invited us into their home, never quite knowing how that statement would be received. Only a few days before, while at a local event, an elderly, church going woman had said, "What you do is the devil's work!" Then almost without taking another breath and reaching across the table to take my hand had asked, "Will you do a reading for me?!"

Our hosts were gracious, with smiles and handshakes all around but there was a somber, almost palpable unease. Unknown to me, a very dear friend had passed away only days before, and now it seemed, they feared death might come calling at their door as well!

"Casandra will do a reading for you!" I heard my man excitedly say.

"Oh, that's not necessary," replied the husband. "I don't really believe in all that stuff anyway!"

"Oh, c'mon, what harm can it do?" his wife, said as she got up to get him paper and pen.

"Here, you take notes. You're good at that!'"

"Well, that's a first!" he chuckled. "My wife telling me I'm good at something."

The tension eased somewhat. They had been married many years and obviously enjoyed their verbal sparring.

Seated in a roomy rocking chair, arms stubbornly folded across his chest, pencil and pad on his lap as instructed, he fixed his eyes somewhat defiantly on his wife as I went into a light trance.

"You'll have a good decade." The reading began. There will be health challenges, but you will be fine." Then came a direct question.

"Have you been diagnosed with breast cancer?" I asked this total stranger. "It is the disease of resentment you know." My source seemed to feel it was important she know.

"Yes," came her soft reply.

Again came my reassurance. "You'll be fine."

Next a 'body scan' revealed she would have problems with her vision in the future. Five years later she had cataract surgery on both eyes. Her reading concluded with advice to walk more -good advice for anyone - to prevent a possible blood clot in her leg. This has yet to manifest and may never as she does keep active.

After a brief pause the energy shifted to childhood events.

"Great anger here, something so traumatic you are not over it yet and it is affecting your health even to this day. I 'see' fire trucks, police cars and traffic. A tragedy, a great loss! Your husband later fills the role of your absent father."

"Yes, yes" was all she would say.

As I was given no more detail about the event, I moved on and ended her reading once again with the phrase, 'a good decade ahead!'

"Now, it's your turn," she said to her husband and with that, my eyes still closed and in trance, I turned and asked him to repeat his name.

Information came flooding in. Some individuals are easier to 'read' than others. Because of the trauma she had suffered, she had been more guarded. Her husband seemed an open book.

"You were born in another country," I began. "There was a lot of fear and noise going on around you. You used to cover your ears to block out the frightening sounds. You met your wife here when you were both young and have been together for a long time. You took over as her father."

Then his body scan revealed, "You also will be fine. You have received some upsetting news about your health, but you also will be alright. But wait, there is something strange here. There is a pain presenting. It begins in your jaw and crosses your body to the other side passing over your heart. It worries you deeply and you have been to several doctors, but it has never been explained."

With that statement, I felt the room go very quiet.

"It is nothing -nothing to worry about -just your body reacting to an old injury." I added.

My eyes still closed, without any verbal or visual feedback, I simply moved on in my reading. I have learned to say whatever I receive no matter how implausible it may seem. It's called trust.

With these final statements the energy began to fade and I opened my eyes to see a man, seated in a comfy rocking chair, arms now by his side, mouth hanging open.

"I think you might have nailed it," my man said.

Now, it was time for me to learn what had been going on in this couple's life prior to this snowy December night.

Both just diagnosed with cancer within weeks of one another - she with breast, he with prostrate - she was to undergo treatment immediately; he was to be monitored – a wait and see approach.

There was more. At the age of fourteen, after speaking with her father on the phone minutes before, she had opened the front door to the knock of a uniformed police officer.

Her father had just been killed in a car accident.

"That's a shock you never get over," she said. "I was filled with rage just like you said. Life took him from me just when I needed him the most. I adored him..." her voice trailed off.

As for the rest of the reading –let's just say it made a believer out of a skeptic!

They had met while in high school. Her family had moved to his town after her father's death and being a bit older, her husband had been a big part of her growing up.

And yes, he had been born in Belgium, a young child during the war with bombs going off pretty much over his head.

"But, how did you know about that pain?" he asked. "I have never told anyone about that!"

"I think that's what she's good at," my man said rather drolly. "Knowing things she's not supposed to know – isn't that what psychics do?" He laughed!

As for death knocking at their door – as of this writing in 2013, now in their seventies, he has had surgery to remove his prostrate and she has weathered yet another scare regarding colon cancer and the comforting phrase, "you'll be fine" has remained true. A good decade; death not yet due at their door!

TRUISM: "Remain calm. See spirit as your true source —-always. When things are difficult ask your higher power for help—always!" Casandra

AMAZING ADVENTURE #37

BREAKFAST IN NEW ENGLAND

2008.
This is a true story.

It sounded like a grand plan. A new friend I had met on a singles' cruise owned a centuries old home in a quaint little New England town and **she** wanted me to visit. You were thinking I had met a man on my singles' cruise weren't you? I had met many, as I had taken several cruises, but none were as right for me as my 'dragonfly day man' but that is another story.

We would drive down and stay a few days. I had never been to New England in autumn with its vermillion coloured rolling hills, tiny hamlets and quaint covered bridges and it seemed like the perfect place to be. Besides her roomy home oozed history, she said, the village was filled with awesome antiques and her address was Sunny Valley Lane! What could be better!

It did not disappoint. Standing on the wrap around porch complete with comfy rocking chairs, one was a little awed by four stately white wooden pillars stretching all the way up to support the portico. Large and spacious, it had been a grand home in its day, built in the late

1600's, by a politician from an historic family. A family which would go on to boast magistrates, legislators, judges and even a president!

My friend, Gale -I always thought the name suited her for you couldn't help but be aware of her energy as she 'blew' into a room- had purchased this lovely old rambling house several years before and turned it into a busy and successful bed and breakfast.

Bored with that, she was now renovating the house and creating apartments. If she stayed single much longer, we joked, she could fill the house with other 'old maids'. 'A seniors home for singles', complete with your own rocking chair on the porch!' was how we would market it. The topic sent us into gales of laughter -excuse the pun - by our third glass of wine as my patient, 'dragon fly day' man simply smiled and nodded.

When it was time to turn in she escorted us to our second story bedroom. She pulled me aside and whispered, "Remember what we talked about before you came? Can you do it tonight?"

It seemed that Sunny Valley Road had a problem. Her name was Clara, a ghost who was in the habit of wandering the halls at night frightening the B&B guests! How her name had come to be known, I would love to say is to be another story, but that bit of information had not been told nor did I think to ask it.

I had been requested to contact her and to politely ask her to leave. There it was, Gale wanted me to perform an exorcism even before breakfast!

"Not tonight. I'm too tired. I'll deal with Clara tomorrow." I said as headed into the large, spacious bedroom complete with antique furniture and the requisite uneven sloping wooden floor!

That's what I thought!

No sooner was I snuggled in under the down comforter, listening to my man softly snore, than I felt it - .a short tug on my wrist. I knew who was standing by the bed. I am psychic.

"Clara, I'm too tired tonight. We'll talk tomorrow," I said without opening my eyes.

Have I mentioned that even though I am a medium and converse with those on the other side, I often choose not to see them? Call me chicken, but I'm just not ready to have them popping up in front of me.

When I felt her energy leave, I went peacefully back to sleep.

The next day dawned full of plans, side trips, shopping, meals and conversation and with no thought of Clara.

She did give us a reason to laugh that night though. As we were getting ready for bed, my man was in the small ensuite washroom brushing his teeth and because, as I have mentioned already, the floors in this very old house were uneven, with a creak, the bathroom door swung closed and hit him right in the bare butt!

I had never seen him move as fast as he flew by me diving in under the covers!

In the wee hours of the morning, Clara came once again. The same jostle of my wrist and I gave the same response. "Tomorrow for sure," I sleepily promised.

Early on the last day of our visit, I was in the shower, but not alone! Clara's energy suddenly filled the small space. Her words began pouring through my brain.

They were coming so fast I knew I would not remember it all so I flew out of the shower, naked and wet, past my jaw dropped man and said, "I need a pen!"

I was busy writing details when it became clear. Clara had an urgent request I was to pass on to Gale.

Taking a few deep breaths to get into a relaxed state, I sat on the side of the bed and began a new, calmer telepathic conversation with Clara.

"What is it you want to ask," I said.

"I need to find my baby son," she said. "I want Gale to go to the grave yard and find where he is buried so I can go see him."

Stunned, I drew in a deep breath as I made sense of what I had just heard and slowly replied, "But Clara you can see your baby son anytime you want. He's there on the other side with you. Just go to the light, Clara. He's there waiting for you."

There was a long silence and then came a simple, innocent question.

"Am I dead?" she asked softly.

"Yes, Clara," I replied.

Again a silence followed and then a flood of happy instructions.

"Tell Gale goodbye for me and if she ever needs me to just call for me and I'll come back. I'm going now. Goodbye."

With that her energy left the room and I sat for a few minutes pondering what might have happened to have separated Clara from her baby son and also how was it that a departed soul could not know she was dead?

Slowly my intuition sketched an image of Clara seated in this very room by the open upstairs window, hands folded limply in her lap, eyes staring blankly, and I 'knew!

Suffering postpartum depression, she never saw her baby boy nor knew he had died shortly after his birth. She had left this house without knowing anything about him only to die shortly thereafter herself! No wonder she came back here looking for him.

Later, Gale and I pieced together a likely scenario. From her energy, I knew Clara had given birth late in life and I also felt she had been single and in disgrace. We discovered from our research that the house had been a birthing centre in the 1800's where women came to have their babies.

In the small town cemetery, she found a single grave marked, 'Clara,' but no child's grave nor family name on the stone.

Whether or not I had gotten the details right really didn't matter to me. What did matter was that Clara no longer walked lonely corridors, her request unheard.

Many times when those who have crossed over have been asked what it's like on the other side, I have been given the simple response, "Not much different than where you are!"

Perhaps that can help explain why many of the spirits I encounter, including Clara, seem 'stuck' in this dimension, not knowing they are dead!

TRUISM: "Souls are continually coming to and going from this earthly experience like silver raindrops descending and ascending. I've 'seen' them. However, some choose to evaporate sooner than others!" Casandra

AMAZING ADVENTURE #38

THE FATHER ON THE STAIRS

2009.
This is a true story.

Since my thirties I have been very good at predicting the sex of the unborn child. At first, I would lay my hand upon the abdomen of the expectant mother and I would 'know', but now all I need is a name even if she is half way around the world. It seems the sounds of the letters of their name give off a signature vibration – at least for me, and allows me to 'find' anyone, born or unborn, and 'know' what their life is about, but those are other stories.

People often ask me if, when I meet them on the street or just casually, do I 'know' things about them right away. The answer to that is yes and no.

Most of the time, I wait to be invited 'in' so to speak. In other words, as a psychic and empath, I have learned to shield myself from the cacophony coming from those around me and only receive information when I focus upon them with that intent.

With that said there are also times when 'knowing' hits me right in the face.

My man and I had decided to stop at one of the well known restaurants in my new home town for something to eat. Named after a famous hockey player as so many places are in Canada, it was a bit unusual as it required climbing a flight of stairs to reach the main dining area. It's a tight squeeze for two way traffic and I found myself face to face with a young man perhaps in his mid-thirties. His anguish took my breath away!

I stood frozen for a moment, and then, my companion, who had been a resident of the town for over twenty years and knew everyone, introduced us.

As I took the young man's hand, the reason for his deep emotional pain flashed through my mind and my mouth opened, almost involuntarily, and spoke these words.

"I hope you won't think me forward or crazy," I began hesitantly. "But, did you just loose an unborn child?"

I rushed on before he could respond as he stood opened mouthed in front of me.

"It will be fine. There will be another and soon. The pregnancy will go perfectly – a little girl I think – yes, a girl. The other was not meant to be and is asking you not to be sad." I

I reached out and touched his arm softly as I heard my man's words coming quickly from behind me.

"She's a psychic. I hope you don't mind. She doesn't do this out of the blue very often but she is pretty accurate!" he stammered in my defense.

The young man smiled, murmuring that it was all alright, thanked me and said his goodbye.

Later we were to find out that his mate had indeed just miscarried.

Six months later we once again met our sad young man on the street, but this time he was beaming from ear to ear! They were expecting once again and he was thrilled. And yes, they had a beautiful little girl!

TRUISM: "You always have a choice. Choose kindness –always!" Casandra

AMAZING ADVENTURE #39

A MULTIPLE EGG PRODUCER!

2009.
This is a true story.

The new man in my life, a Dutch Canadian and a business owner, lived in a resort community surrounded by rolling hills and nestled on the shores of a large lake. When he had arrived from a foreign country at the age of twelve, no one seemed able to pronounce his name. It was spelled JEEN, and consequently, not being happy being referred to as a pair of pants, he had simply said, 'call me Wayne', and it had stuck.

However, when I had done some research on him when dating- yes ladies, it's a good idea to check a new man out - many of his friends had referred to him as, "The Doughboy"! It turned out it was because he had owned and operated a bakery for many years - not because he had a lot of money!

We had been dating now for a little over a year. I enjoyed his company, but because he was so different from the men I usually chose, I didn't see any long term possibility in the cards. A visit to a psychic later shook that belief, but that is another story!

For now it was autumn, the west coast was lovely that time of year he said and would I care to join him in a visit to his son and daughter-in-law's who now lived there? An avid traveler, I was happy to go.

A handsome and affable young man met us at the airport. The son resembled the father it seemed.

Our week sped by as the young couple showed us the city sights. The daughter-in-law was a tall, lithe, dark haired, attractive woman with a razor sharp mind. His son's good natured banter and great joy de vie was a perfect balance for her reserved, somewhat serious demeanor.

Happily married now for several years, they appeared to be a great match and very content with their childless, cosmopolitan lifestyle. There had been no talk of starting a family so it was with complete surprise that while casually sipping wine in their apartment one lazy afternoon, I had looked at her slim form and blurted out the following phrase.

"You're a multiple egg producer!"

There it was— a weird, unsolicited pronouncement if ever there was one!

Stunned silence followed as we all stared at one another.

"That was a real conversational bomb!" I thought to myself! Well, here goes nothing. I'd better finish what I'd started. There was more.

"You're the mother of twins," was what came out next. "Does anyone in your family have twins?" I asked trying to keep the conversation light.

"Noooooo…," was all she could stammer. "We have never thought about the possibility of twins. They aren't in either of our families, but we have been discussing starting a family soon."

Well, there it was.

"Are you always right with your predictions?" she asked a little nervously.

We all laughed as I simply said, "I'll guess we'll see!"

And we did. Several months later, she conceived and weeks later the beginnings of two tiny lives appeared in the first ultrasound. Twins were indeed on their way.

It appeared they were two baby girls, or perhaps one was just a shy boy, I kept saying for he really wanted a son. If they were the same sex that might mean they had come from only one fertilized egg which had divided and were identical twins, but it was also possible they could have developed from two distinct eggs and be fraternal twins .

Two beautifully healthy, robust little twin girls presented themselves right on schedule. In many ways so similar, but not identical!

As foretold, she had indeed been a 'multiple egg producer' – the mother of fraternal twins!

TRUISM: "If you have money in the bank, in your wallet and spare change somewhere in a dish, you are among the top 8% of the worlds' wealthy." Stumbled upon.com

AMAZING ADVENTURE #40

THE KILLING PLACE

2010.
This is a true story.

I have a daughter who chose to live in South Africa. An avid advocate of animal rights, she went on holiday where she might be surrounded by the beauty and grace of the wilderness and fell in love – both with Africa and a man!

I was about to meet both for the first time.

It was to be a grand, month long adventure! She and her new man were busy making plans to ensure that our little party of three -the man in my life, my seven year old granddaughter and I - would see as much of South Africa and Zimbabwe as possible!

She had met him several years before while vacationing at one of the wild life reserves he owned. A white, German native of Zimbabwe, he and his family had been forced from their land while he was only a young man. Expelled forcibly from a country he loved, he then became a citizen of South Africa, attended pharmacological college in Johannesburg and went on to own his own pharmacy as well as partner in the ownership of wildlife reserves and camps. He had long ago fallen love with the grace and beauty of the wilderness and more recently the grace and beauty of my daughter it appeared.

Our flight included a brief lay over in Amsterdam with a quick trip through Skippol airport and the purchase of a brightly coloured pair of wooden shoes for my granddaughter. We would have loved to spend more time there as my new man had emigrated from Holland when he was twelve years of age and had never returned in all of the nearly fifty years he had lived in Canada.

Back on the KLM flight headed for Johannesburg, my lovely young granddaughter decided she needed to use the washroom. This was her first airplane flight ever and I thought she was handling it remarkable well. The stewardesses had been most attentive thus far, the plane large and roomy, with excellent service.

Seated on the commode in the closet commonly called a washroom on airplanes, Missy- as I liked to call her- her feet swinging comfortably, ankles crossed surveyed her surroundings chirped, "Grandma, I think I like this flying thing!"

As we exited the washroom we stopped to look out through a round window at the clouds passing below us and, a stewardess overheard her ask, "where are we now, Grandma?'

"Well, we'll just have to ask the captain now, won't we," was her response as she lifted a telephone receiver from the wall beside her.

"Captain," she began. "We have a lovely young passenger here who would like to know just where we are. Would you like to speak with her?" she asked as she handed the phone to my granddaughter.

Needless to say, my granddaughter floated back to her seat convinced that flying truly was the way to travel!

We arrived in Johannesburg, tired and in need of a shower! Almost twenty hours en route left me wondering whether I still had the stamina for travel at my age!

I love my youngest daughter with all my heart and I had missed her terribly. It is a very good thing that my love for her is great enough to set her free for after what I witnessed in Africa, I can only say it would not be a life I would have chosen for her, but that is this story!

Her home was encased with thick brick walls, topped with barbed wire. We had to pass through a security gate to enter the property. There were bars on every window and door– no screens – just bars. To enter through the main door, an iron gate must first be unlocked and then the sturdy wooden door behind it. She informed me as we entered the house, that many of their friends also had a locked gate barring the entrance into their master bedrooms - rather like a last ditch panic room in case of home invasions.

And then there were her dogs – three of them. She had always had pets, but now these dogs served a more sinister function. They were her protectors. Strays, they had been rescued from the animal shelter where she now worked as a veterinary technician and they were devoted to her safety. She never travelled without her pit bull crossbred with jaws that could crush a man's skull. Used as a breeding bitch for the dog fights, the animal had been terribly abused by the blacks in the townships.

I lay in bed that first night, listening to the sounds of barking all around, for all households in that white neighbourhood had guard dogs, and wondered, "Who really was imprisoned in this country?" For it was the white population who lived behind the bars!

This was only the beginning!

My daughter had adapted to her new way of life. Fulfilled by her work with the poor and disenfranchised both animal and human, she was doing what she had been born to do. I knew that. She was in her right place. I, on the other hand, had never felt more out of place!

Always conscious of my responsibility to keep my granddaughter safe, I never let her out of my sight. While shopping in the local mall, I watched as the many black faces stared at us -some with curiosity, some with undisguised hatred.

South Africa now is almost ninety per cent black. I learned first hand how it feels to be a minority. Many whites share my discomfort and have been trying for years to leave. I was shocked to learn that a citizen cannot leave South Africa even on a holiday without permission from the government!

My daughter's man, because he is a wealthy businessman, would have to leave everything behind him. Even with that, he told me, only five per cent of his graduating class still remains in SA.

And yet, even though I felt terrorized by the people there, I came to understand why my daughter and her man wanted to stay.

Once away from the depressing gray decay of a city that rapes the earth for its minerals, Joburg, as it is called, was behind us and before us lay the most magnificent vistas I have ever witnessed. The country spreads itself before you as a jewel. Its colours, shapes and sparkling sun splashed blue skies can take your breath away. And then there are the animals! I never knew a giraffe was so majestic, its skin rich brown and vermillion orange - that a leopard's eyes were piercing yellow as they blinked from a rich brown and lemon coloured face. A pod of hippos sound like chain saws as they yawn, their wide mouths warning you that you've come too close! And the elephants-they splash and play along the riverbanks, moving majestically and mightily on their way when done.

We saw all the 'big five' as they call them in Africa - elephant, lion, leopard, rhinoceros, water buffalo - but the wildest thing I 'saw' was not the animals!

We had been travelling now for days, headed north to Zimbabwe. My daughter's man was in charge of this expedition and as he negotiated our border crossing into the country of his birth, he instructed us not to speak as our Canadian accents could cause more unnecessary delays. We left our vehicle, an ancient but reliable Volkswagen van, referred to as a 'kombi' in the care of a young, thin boy for the price of a few coins and an apple and joined a long line of others waiting for clearance into Zimbabwe. As I glanced back nervously wondering if we would ever see our vehicle in one piece again, my daughter reassured me that our young man had been paid handsomely enough!

Guards with guns were everywhere! They lined the roads as we entered this civil war torn, bankrupt country. We met guns often as our route was lined with 'check points' where a toll was paid. It was no more than a black man or woman seated beside an old barrel or pylon in the middle of the road with hand outstretched. Further off the road, was usually a small shack with armed guards slouched against it.

When I asked what would happen if we didn't pay a toll which was no more than government sanctioned extortion, my daughter's man calmly answered, "They'd shoot."

All along the way, my daughter would ask whoever was driving to stop when we saw women or children walking on the road. They'd look at us hesitantly at first, afraid to approach our vehicle for fear of being abducted or worse, but as my granddaughter's young arms appeared from it's window full of 'sweeties' they would come running, full of smiles. You would have thought we had given them the world as they grinned up at us, lollipop clutched in their hands. For the women, she had mielle meal', or what we knew as corn meal, in five pound sacks and as they received them tears ran down their tired faces. "Thank you, thank you. God bless you!' We heard that more than I ever wanted to.

We seemed never to stop for gas or supplies. There was nothing in the stores to buy so we carried our own. I had never seen toilet paper displayed and purchased a single roll at a time, nor had I ever carried it into the bush as often.

As the hours and miles of deserted countryside passed, I asked once as we witnessed a bus which had careened off the road now perched precariously on the side of a cliff being hauled to safety by another vehicle, "what would happen if we ever broke down?" There was certainly no calling triple A here!

"I'd just make a plan" he said. "I did compulsory military service." He went on to tell of the time his truck had had a broken axle.

"We just made one from a tree we cut down. It worked so well that we left it a couple of months before we replaced it."

He told this story as if it was nothing unusual for in this part of the world self reliance appeared to be mandatory for survival.

We were on our way to what had been in this country's day of the 'great white hunter', a five star resort, called Matumbo.

Miles and miles of a one lane dirt trail filled with deep ruts and jutting boulders passed beneath our vehicle as it veered and jarred its way along. My daughter's man, our South African guide, was in his glory – this was just the type of driving he relished, often travelling making his own road!

Dusk was descending. We were sweaty, hot, tired and thirsty as finally we arrived at the resort's entrance gates. Pulling up beside a grass roofed hut, stepping out to greet us was the biggest, tallest, blackest man I have ever seen. He wore a large white bib apron over his clothes.

He rumbled a greeting and our guide responded in English asking if they could accommodate us.

"We have no power. No way to cook. We cannot feed you."

It appeared we had been greeted by the cook! Power outages were common in this country or as my daughter explained, "In Zimbabwe, nothing works!"

We explained that all we wanted was accommodation for the night and asked how much?

"For five of you – five hundred American dollars," was the reply.

"Outrageous!" was our guide's answer.

He turned to us and said, "We'll head back. I know another place further down on the main road. It's way too much to pay here!"

Further down on the main road! It was at least four hours of slow going over rough road in the dark to get there!

"Grandma will pay!" I shouted from the back of the kombi! At that I point I would have paid almost anything.

Our accommodations were stunning! Missy, my companion and I were led to our own private thatched roof villa perched amid rolling hills of pink, rounded rock looking out over miles of more of the same. My daughter and her man also had their own villa connected to ours by a path that meandered over the rocks and rivaled our view.

"You will be called to dinner by the drums," our guide informed us. The power had returned long enough for the cook to prepare our meal.

My granddaughter and I were alone in our room unpacking a few things when she came and wrapped her now sun browned arms around me.

"Grandma, I don't like it here. This place scares me," she said, her eyes wide.

This was unusual as it was the very first time in our two weeks in Africa she had exhibited any other emotion other than an incredible sense of adventure and fun! She had loved every minute of our trip!

"Can I push my bed next to yours, Grandma? You'll sleep with me here tonight, won't you? Please don't leave me alone here. I don't like this place."

I hugged her and told her Grandma would never let anything bad happen to her and I meant it.

Darkness and drums called us to a large outdoor eating area. The dining table overlooked miles of uninhabited African wilderness from its vantage point atop a large flat-topped rock. Torches surrounded us with the glow of firelight as we were served silently and expertly by the same black man who had greeted us at the gate.

What we ate, I cannot remember for the food was not nearly as remarkable as the canopy of stars above us, the sounds of the African night and my complete and utter sense of being at the end of the world!

True to my word, my granddaughter slept with her bed pushed next to mine. I left it until the last possible moment to extinguish the candle light filling the walls of our room with soft eerie shadows of the many animal trophies from past hunts that adorned the stone walls.

I slept fitfully. I hated to admit it, but I did not like this place either. Perhaps the best way to describe it was that it was fiercely beautiful. There was an unsettled, restless, dark energy about this place of unparalleled physical beauty.

Sweat covered my body as I awoke gasping in the close night air. A horrific fear of being kidnapped and raped surged through me. What if my daughter and her man, our guide, were taken? What would we do here? How could we be safe?

Crazy thoughts and images of unspeakably violent acts surged through my brain.

"This is nuts!" I thought to myself as got up to light the candle once again. I looked over at my granddaughter's soft sleeping face. My man also slept soundly beside me. Was I going crazy?

For the rest of that long night, I watched the flicker of that candle and convinced myself the images of women and children being kidnapped, raped and tortured also flickering through my brain were simply my own exhaustion and sense of fear for my granddaughter's safety in what I perceived to be an unsafe land.

As dawn broke, I dressed and quietly left our villa in search of some morning air and perhaps a hot cup of tea. Hopefully, water boiled and tea brewed in this strange place!

I seated myself at the great dining table atop the same flat rock as the night before. There was no sign of our cook. There was no sign of anyone until an official looking middle aged black man in a crisp green uniform appeared by my side. He introduced himself as the manager of the resort and apologized for not greeting us the night before.

My tea was ordered, appeared and the manger seemed in the mood to talk. I sipped and listened and as I listened more, I sipped less.

For what he had to tell me I already knew.

He described the atrocities of the civil war, some of which had occurred on this very spot. The blacks had expelled the white farmers from what had been called, the 'bread basket of Africa', Zimbabwe, and unable to maintain the sophisticated equipment and methods of farming, over time had drastically reduced the production of food. As scarcity settled in, black turned upon black.

"It was festival time here." He explained. "They had set up the huge vats for brewing beer along the river banks. The attack came swiftly. Women and children were carried off, some killed where they stood, children thrown into the bubbling vats of beer to be cooked alive, pregnant women's bellies slashed open and the fetuses throw into the river. It was attempted genocide – the desire to destroy all traces of one another and in the process all we succeeded in doing was destroying ourselves."

"We are trying now," he said, "to bring back the white tourist, but it is a very slow process to build their trust."

At that point he turned to see the rest of my companions coming to join me so he ended our conversation with a slight bow and the words, "May you have a pleasant day, Ma'am and may God forgive us all."

As my granddaughter settled herself into my lap and breakfast was being served, I looked across the table where our large black cook was standing, waiting. His stare was firmly fixed upon the back of my companion's fair head, his eyes filled with hatred. It had not escaped me that he had seen my man's blue eyes, fair skin and heard the trace of an accent.

Perhaps it had been unwise to travel with a Dutchman in a place where many of his countrymen had imposed their will for so long.

The horror my granddaughter felt and I 'saw' will never leave my memory.

Indeed, may God forgive us all.

TRUISM: "Take time for silence each day. We have two ears and one mouth. The wise use them in that proportion." Casandra

AMAZING ADVENTURE #41
THE PROMISE

2012.
This is a true story.

I awoke with a start – sucking in my breath. The bedroom was silent and dark around me, but I 'knew' someone was there!

Let me back up a bit. As you may know from reading my stories, I am a psychic. Thus one might believe that I 'see' spirits all the time. Not so! Although I am often called to communicate with those who have departed, I rarely choose to see them! I 'hear' their thoughts in my head, sometimes accompanied by visual images of objects or even floral scent which help to verify who they are, but they don't present themselves – at least not to me! Obviously, I am just too big a chicken to see them!

So it was on this warm Florida spring night in my bedroom, I had the uncomfortable sense I was not alone.

Eyes tightly shut, I repeated the Unity prayer of protection – the light of God surrounds me – the light of God protects me – over and over in my head. Finally, my fear eased and I spoke out loud, apologetically, "you'll just have to forgive me, I'm just not ready to see you!"

With that, I felt the energy in the room change and I was able to drift off to sleep.

The next morning, cup of tea in hand, seated comfortably in my favourite chair on the lanai, I prepared to do my morning meditation.

Relaxed and centered, the question of who had 'visited' me the night before came into my thoughts.

"It was your father," came the answer. "He just came to say hello."

My father has been deceased now for many years but, even though I have never 'seen' him, I have often felt his presence. Pleased by the prospect that he had 'stopped by', smiling to myself, I went into the kitchen for another cup of tea. There on the counter, my Blackberry was buzzing with an incoming email. Picking it up, I saw that it was from my youngest daughter who was now living in South Africa.

"You'll never guess who came to visit me last night!" it read. "It was Granddad!"

"I woke up out of a sound sleep at two in the morning thinking it was an intruder! But as I sat up ready to defend myself, the dark shadowy outline of a man's face didn't move. I knew then it must be a spirit because it didn't react to me. As I looked closer, I could see the distinct outline of his profile – you know that crazy brush cut he had – it was him alright! I lay back down in bed and said, "Hi Granddad, nice of you to come by."(Unlike me, she is not a big chicken when it comes to seeing spirits – but that is another story!)The room filled with this incredible sense of peace and I went back to sleep." she wrote. "It was really cool- I felt really loved and protected."

Well Dad, I thought to myself, I guess you really got around last night!

But, as I came to believe later, his visits might have had another purpose as well.

A few weeks before, my aunt, my father's sister-in-law had passed away. She had lived mainly as a recluse most of her life, but had been very fond of my father. When he had died, my aunt had told us he had come to visit her and as she 'saw' him standing in the doorway of her apartment he had said to her, "It's beautiful here. You should come with me. It's time."

Stubbornly clinging to what many might call a sheltered life, she had answered. "No, I'm scared. I'm not ready yet."

To that, she had reported he 'said' to her. "Alright, when you are, I promise I will come and get you." And with that he was gone.

Laughing, delighted that Dad was 'visiting' I was busy relating these coincidences to my oldest daughter who is a teacher in the same town where my aunt lived and she became rather quiet.

"You know, Mom" she began. "I asked Auntie to give me a sign after she passed and she said she would if she could. You know how musical she was, so I expected that I might 'hear' her play one of her instruments for me."

"Well," she went on, "the same night Granddad came to visit you and sis, my iPod went off at two in the morning. It has never done that before and it was playing this beautiful music! I thought it was really bizarre but didn't think anything of it until now. Do you think that Granddad and Auntie were just out having a ball visiting everyone? You know he did promise to come and get her!"

"So he did," I said.

He always was a man of his word.

TRUISM: "If you carried a bag with you and each time you did not forgive a perceived transgression, either your own or another's, you put a stone in it, how heavy would it be? Forgiveness is the gift you give yourself." Casandra

AMAZING ADVENTURE #42

THE BOY ON THE STAIRS

2012.
This is a true story.

I had just finished presenting a seminar at a spa and retreat centre in a small town. Vine covered medieval style buildings set beside a tranquil lake, a nearby labyrinth, horse stables, lush herb garden and gurgling stream below my turreted upper balcony all contributed to my delight and fantasy that Merlyn the great wizard might indeed appear beneath my window at any moment. For you see, my topic had been, 'Developing Your Psychic Powers'!

Relaxed and happy as I checked out, I chatted with the front desk clerk. All the staff had such wonderfully appropriate names it seemed for Angela, a true angel, had arranged my stay and now Sherry, also the name of an alcoholic drink commonly referred to as spirits, was about to engage me in a discussion of the very same – spirits that is!

"I think you'll definitely be coming back!" She chirped. "Your workshop and psychic readings were very well received!"

"Well, when I do, would it be possible to have a different room?" I asked. "Room 101 sure was a busy place, if you know what I mean!"

Sherry tilted her head to one side and smiled.

"Oh, I see you've met some of our non paying guests!" she laughed.

I went on to tell her about the several visits I had experienced over the four nights I had spent in Room 101.

Cozy in the great bed under a down duvet my first evening I had drifted off to sleep only to be awakened with the definite thought that someone was in the room. Having experienced this many times before, I simply asked, "Who are you?"

At that point a mental image of a middle aged, grey haired woman in a long flowing dressing gown flashed before my eyes. Appearing very despondent and somewhat confused, she blinked at me almost if she was wondering where I had come from!

To some it may appear that what I said next was heartless, but I have learned through many experiences with these phenomena, it is best to be direct.

"Dear, do you know you are dead?" I said as kindly as I could.

She continued to stare silently, only blinking.

"You can go to the light now. There are loved ones who are waiting to greet you. Your time here is done." I spoke softly, reassuring her.

With that she turned slowly, moving into the light that was now filling the room and slowly faded from my consciousness.

I rolled over and went back to sleep.

Each of the next two nights similar visitors, often bringing the energy of confusion, pain or anger were told the very same thing with the very same result. All were healed by turning their attention to an all enveloping light that would fill the room.

On my last night, I awoke to 'see' a sad faced young boy, dressed only in trousers, standing quietly by my bed. Before I could speak, he slowly turned to reveal his bare back.

Shock shuddered through my body as I looked upon deeply scarred flesh.

Compassion for this suffering young soul flooded my consciousness and I whispered softly, "It's alright now. You are safe. Go to the light for there are many there who love you. God bless you."

With that he turned and was wordlessly gone.

When I finished recounting this last experience, Sherry simply said, "Oh, I see you've met the young boy who burned to death here years ago. Many guests have seen him sitting on the stairs in this very reception area."

My jaw did drop a bit, I admit, and Sherry and I both stared at each other and said at the same time, "OOOHHH, I've got goose bumps!

I'm returning to the spa again soon and I will surely ask if the young boy has returned to sit on the stairs, but that will be another story!

TRUISM: "Say what you mean. Mean what you say. The truth will set you free." Casandra

AMAZING ADVENTURE #43

SIX THOUSAND AND FORTY SIX LITTLE BLUE BALLS

2013.
This is a true story.

Do you believe in a psychic gene?" my daughter asked.

"A psychic what? You mean something that jumps out of a magic lamp when you rub it?" I replied. I was having fun with her and she knew it.

"No, that's a genie! You know. Do you think psychic abilities are inherited?"

"Yes", was my short response.

The long one was, "Why do you ask?"

I, of course, already knew. I had been psychic since my early twenties, some forty plus years at this point. She had had a psychic insight.

She proceeded to tell me what had occurred.

"Well ….," she hesitated. "You know we were in away this past week and your grandson and I were at this convention centre and there was this display promoting Scotland. As we went over for a closer look, there was a huge tank filled with hundreds of small blue balls with a plastic Loch Ness monster nestled neatly among them!"

I couldn't help but think her choice of words was appropriate—Nessie was nestled!

She went on, "Your grandson of course was intrigued. You know how inquisitive an eight year old is and you know what a born teacher I am, so of course I thought it was a perfect opportunity for a mathematics lesson! As we walked toward the tank, it was as if a ball of light hit my forehead and a whooshing roar went past my ears. I 'saw' the numerals 6046 flash before my eyes. That's strange I thought to myself –really weird!"

She continued, "I shrugged it off and we set about estimating the number of tiny blue balls filling the tank. We guessed at the dimensions of the bottom of the container, drew a grid, and counted the approximate number in one square and then multiplied by the number of squares we thought were in the tank. It was great fun and great mathematics! When the answer came out as six thousand and forty, my skin goose bumped! All the time we had been having such fun doing our calculations, I had been thinking about how much I loved to travel and wouldn't it be wonderful to take a trip to Scotland! We hadn't noticed the sign announcing the draw —the prize was two round trip tickets to Scotland, entry fee, five dollars!"

"What the heck," I thought. "We only need one guess to win so down on the slip of paper went the number that had flashed before my eyes minutes earlier. Six thousand and forty six was our entry. I handed the slip of paper to the elderly gentleman conducting the draw and as we walked away I heard the lady beside him ask quietly, 'Do we have a lucky entry?' We turned to see him bend down and whisper something in her ear as we giggled and I thought, 'Could it possibly be?'"

"Driving home the next day, when I answered my cell phone, a thick Scottish burr asked if he was speaking to the mother and son who had been at the convention centre this past weekend. We answered that indeed it was and yes we had entered their contest and then took a breath long enough to hear him say, 'Well, you've won!'"

"Do you think I should go and buy some lottery tickets, Mom?" she asked.

I laughed and wondered what the universe had in store for a psychic daughter and a curious grandson on a Scottish adventure?

Will that be another story?

TRUISM: "Watch your thoughts. Thoughts become words; words become actions; actions become habits; habits become character; character defines destiny!" Margaret Thatcher

AMAZING PSYCHIC STORY #44

THE BIRTHDAY GIFT

2013.
This is a true story.

I chose the quote by Margaret Thatcher's to introduce this story for in so many ways my aunt, whom this story is about, was so like the Iron Maiden.

On a bleak January day my mother's sister chose to pass. I say chose for indeed she did. It was not suicide. No, it was more a decision to affirm she was more than her body, but I am getting ahead of my story.

At the Memorial Service, my cousin, who is about my age, seemed anxious to talk.

"Casandra," she said as she took my arm and steered me away to a private corner. "I have something about Mom's passing I want to discuss with you. I know you are a medium and I know you will be interested in what happened after Mom died."

What follows is the story she recounted to me.

"As you know Mom passed away on January 15th this year and being her oldest daughter and having lived so close to her all these years, I was devastated. One night after her passing I had such a vivid dream. In her apartment surrounded by all her things, in anguish I called out to the empty walls the question I knew had no answer, but I needed to ask anyway!"

"Why did you have to die, Mom?" I wailed.

And then she was there with me just as she had always been.

"It was my time – my choice." She answered softly.

"But, why now. It will be so hard now. Valentine's Day will soon be here and there will be no birthday card from you. Every year –I have them all – the beautiful cards you sent to your Valentine's baby!"

"You will have your birthday gift this year, I promise. It can come from anywhere you know – even heaven." With that she was gone and so was my dream.

February 14th arrived and even though I was vacationing in warm, sunny Arizona I was despondent. My husband was to be golfing during the day and he encouraged me to go shopping with some friends. While at lunch I overheard two older ladies discussing an excursion they were planning that afternoon - a visit to church in the desert. For some unknown reason, I felt compelled to ask them about their plans. They felt compelled to invite me to come along. So it was that I soon found myself travelling into the Tucson desert with two complete strangers!

We arrived at a beautiful, small, white washed adobe church. Designated as an historical site, it was no longer used for weekly worship. As I wandered through the building examining the display cases filled with rich robes, leather bound bibles, portraits and rosaries, it dawned on me that this was a Catholic church. My mother had raised us as Catholics as she had been born into a large Catholic family of twelve children.

As I sat pondering why I was here, I felt an overwhelming sense of her presence.

"I was a nun in another life." My mother's voice said in my head. "I was known as Sister Delores. You see. I didn't forget your birthday. I am here with you now. I am always with you."

"I left that small church with a smile in my heart." My cousin went on to tell the rest of her story.

"My birthday passed and so did my vacation. Later, at home I received a call from my sister who now lives in India. Here's what she had to tell me."

"You know," she said. "The strangest thing happened to me on your birthday. Mom came to me in a dream that night. She was young and beautiful, but she was dressed as a nun! She said she was a nun and in the dream she removed part of her body and she said, 'I am no longer of the flesh!'"

My cousin continued. "There was a long moment of silence on the phone and a few goose bumps as the two of us processed what had just been discussed. You know, Casandra, they didn't know what to list as Mom's cause of death. Being a nurse, I had insisted they run all the tests on her when she started becoming forgetful. She passed with flying colours – they could find nothing physically wrong with her. She had always been so sharp, so witty and strong minded. I think she decided that if her mind was deteriorating, she was just going to take her body out! It took us awhile to figure out she had just stopped eating months before her death. She had hidden the evidence of self-starvation well."

We ended our lengthy chat, laughing, reminiscing about her mother, my aunt. We talked about her strength of character, her determination to raise her six children to be strong and independent, her wit, her love of life and her choice to leave this earth. She had certainly lived her life her way and had also ended it her way! Surrounded by her loving family, she had said goodbye to each one and had given and received forgiveness from all.

My aunt's name you ask? Everyone knew her as Doris, but she had been baptized, Delores Marie, born 1926.

My research revealed there had indeed a nun named Sister Maria Delores who lived from 1848 to 1918. Born in Spain, she did spend time in the Americas. Because of her work with the poor, Pope John Paul 11 declared her life's work heroic and in 2002 she was declared a saint.

Coincidence?—probably. But with my aunt's terrific love of a good joke, I am not surprised she chose to appear as a saint! Nevertheless, with the sheer force of her will, her spirit triumphed over her flesh. She died with dignity and when she chose! Add to that her ability to communicate with loved ones after death, and nothing would surprise me, but that would be another story!

TRUISM: "May you always be awake and aware; your experience here peaceful, pleasurable and prosperous, but not permanent and when the time comes may you take the exit marked, 'Forgiveness'." Casandra

AMAZING ADVENTURE #45

THE WRONG WAY OUT

2013.
This is a true story.

I chose to place this story near the end of my book even though it occurred several years ago for its subject matter is the ultimate ending – death. Or perhaps, I should say, the way some souls choose to exit life.

The title suggests a right and a wrong way to do this. Let me be clear here. Never in hundreds of readings have I ever encountered any form of judgment other than self judgment, but for souls who have chosen the exit marked, 'self-destruct', if suffering is not the desired outcome, then indeed it is, 'the wrong way out'.

It was the mid 1990's and the man I was reading was the youngest, now adult, brother of a close friend and mentor. In my mind's eye, he 'appeared' to me as a young boy of six or seven clad only in pajamas, foot frozen on a stairway, his descent into a basement room halted, a loud bang still ringing in his ears, and then nothing – a blank memory – complete inability to recall anything further.

Let me begin at the beginning. My friend and mentor and I, in a romantic relationship now for about six months, had decided on a trip together. Walking down the carpeted corridor of our hotel room, I couldn't help but notice, that once again, he was whistling a strangely familiar tune.

"What is that you are always whistling?" I asked,

"Oh, that. I guess I picked it up from my dad. He used to whistle it wherever he went."

"Isn't it called, 'Turn Around Look at Me,'" I asked?

"Ya," he replied as he sang some lyrics. I think it goes like this.

"There is someone walking behind you, turn around, look at me. There is someone to love and guide you, turn around look at me."

His voice trailed off as he saw a strange expression cross my face. The hair was standing up on the back of my neck.

"Your dad's spirit is here with us now, "I said softly. "He wants to tell you something."

In the hotel room, connecting fully with his father's energy, I felt drawn visually to the edge of a deep, dark pit. Standing on the precipice, I stared down into an opening choked with tangled, thick, thorny vines designed to shred whoever might try to escape. From its depth's came these words.

"Tell my son I am proud of him and I ask his forgiveness."

Gut wrenching sobs filled my ears. They came from the son who had picked up the shattered pieces of a family after the tragedy. The oldest of five children, my friend had been married and living away from home on the fateful Christmas Eve his younger brother had stood frozen on the stairway. The youngest child, he had been left with his father while everyone else had gone Christmas shopping.

To this day, he has no conscious memory of that night's events.

His father was found slumped over, rifle by his hand, fatally shot in the head. An untreated manic depressive, who often medicated with alcohol, the many doctors his wife had taken him to saying, "He's not a drunk. He's sick!" had been unable to help him.

With no successful treatment for manic depression at that time suicide had seemed the only way out.

His words went on, "Tell him I have forgiven myself and because of that I am free. I will be with him always."

With that his energy faded and I was left with a sobbing man in my arms, a healing begun.

On two other occasions I have connected with a soul who chose the 'wrong exit' and it has been the same.

A deep, dark pit and anguished words filled with regret- deep regret for a wasted opportunity to conquer the pain of misperception. For truly, I believe, we are eternal beings, never destroyed, only to linger in suffering of our own free will. Always forgiveness is the answer - the right way out.

Throughout my life as a 'mystic medium,' this is what I have come to 'know'. The creative force is love. We are one with that energy; our sense of separateness false.

To overcome death, as created and creator is possible. To know this truth sets us free.

TRUISM: "The result of a peaceful mind is kindness." Casandra

AMAZING ADVENTURE #46

LET ME ENTERTAIN YOU!

2013.
This is a true story.

This was to be the last story, but it's not. Perhaps the universe had other plans. There is another, but, this is this one.

For most of my life, as you have now read, I have been fascinated by psychic phenomena. It wasn't always a love affair however. At first I didn't take my abilities seriously, then when they asserted themselves more dramatically, they frightened me, until after many years of sporadic practice, more social acceptance and dramatically accurate predictions, I began to trust this was who I was – a mystic and a medium.

All well and good you say, but to what purpose, I say? Always a practical person, who loves result for effort, and who always desires to prove theories through personal experience, it seemed a cruel twist of fate to have an ability that was in many people's opinion, useless and unverifiable. But there it was. I have learned, the hard way, not to argue with reality.

Ah reality…. That brings me now to another thought. What is 'reality'?

I have read serious authors who state we create our own reality through our thoughts. In other words, 'what we think about – we bring about.' My personal experience has supported this for as an avid and practiced goal setter, through sustained focus and visualization, I have manifested everything in my life I have desired! My belief in this principle is so strong; I find great satisfaction in teaching others how to do the same.

I had everything figured out, I thought, but there was this one nagging experience.

Let me back up a bit. I don't think anyone has to be psychic to see there is a great deal of suffering going on here on earth. And if it is true we create our own reality, there must be an awful lot of people who wish to suffer! If, as some authors suggest, nothing appears in our life unless we have consciously or unconsciously summoned it, our minds must be a bit masochistic wouldn't one think? If we are truly divine beings as so many, including me, teach it just didn't seem to add up.

Let me back up a bit more. I promise there will be a point to all this musing. I refer now to that nagging experience I mentioned earlier.

It happened one night - great movie title but not the title of this story - when I was channeling the Council of One. Every Tuesday night many would come to our office boardroom to receive psychic guidance. My mentor and friend, would field the questions as I sat, eyes closed, in a light trance state giving voice to the knowledge that would land in my mind as complete thought. I never knew what word was coming next. I did my best to interpret mental images and symbols appearing in my mind's eye, but most often it came as a stream of thought, complete in and of itself, without any use of inductive or deductive reasoning on my part. It was as if someone else was thinking with my brain!

There was a lull this particular evening as I sat, eyes closed waiting in a room filled with about thirty individuals, most of whom had already asked their questions of the Council Of One. I heard my friend clear his throat and then he said, "I have one for the Council, Casandra! It's a question I have always wondered about!"

There was a sense of glee in his voice. At last he was to get an answer. He seemed so pleased with himself.

When I heard his question, my heart sank. "Oh no," I thought sarcastically. "Why not ask a hard one?" As you can see, I may have been in touch with enlightened energy, but I was still very human!

"Why did he have to ask that in front of all these people? How can I possibly come up with an answer?" I was panicking.

Deep breath – I took one – that always helped me to remember it wasn't my job to come up with the answer. Go deeper, I thought to myself; turn it over; ask the Council and that was what I did.

"Would you please repeat your question," I asked, slipping into trust and ready to speak whatever came.

"Okay," he said. "Why are we here? What's the purpose of life on this planet?"

"Oh boy," I thought as the answer came fast, clean and clear. "Here goes!" I spoke only two words - no more.

"For entertainment."

That was it - just two simple words!

Can you see now, why this experience has nagged at me all these years?

The group seemed to accept the answer pretty well. No one angrily challenged it; in fact, most nodded their heads in acceptance!

Well, maybe they are living on a different planet than I am," I thought to myself. "Life doesn't seem like it's all that entertaining for so many of us!"

Well, that was then and this is now. Ten years ago that answer came to me so I've had some time to think about it. Lately, I have been doing some reading which suggests what we experience as life on this planet is only an illusion – reality in reality only a dream? As crazy as that may sound, I'm beginning to believe it and here is why. I have experienced that as I change my thinking, I change my life. I have experienced that when I forgive and cease to judge, my world is peaceful no matter what is going on around me. I have experienced that as I let go of my attachment to the physical, I suffer less and less. I have experienced that I am not my mind nor my personality, but so much more. I have come to know and trust what I call my 'higher self' which is my intuitive connection to the creative force. I have come to believe I am immortal energy. I was never created and can never be destroyed for I have always been. Thus, as I have stepped out of my attachment to this life experience, I have truly come to believe, I am living in my own movie and I am the only critic. It matters only to me whether or not it is entertaining. I am always forgiven everything by source energy; I am the prodigal daughter on my way back home. Nothing I say or do in this life matters except as a way of waking up to knowledge that I am one with all that is – not separate - and in forgiving myself for ever believing I was less than whole, I am destined to return home from the theatre in which I have watched my self-made movie!

It's certainly held my attention. It's been a roller coaster ride full of ups and downs, loneliness and romance, joys and sorrows, fear and courage, pleasure and pain, war and peace. What a ride it has been! Kind of like a day at an amusement park. And if it really is only one lifetime of many, and if we can go home whenever we want to an experience of only peace, I guess in that context I can really honestly say –

THAT'S ENTERTAINMENT!!

TRUISM: "Children learn what they live, but your past does not have to be your future." Casandra

AMAZING ADVENTURE #47

WELCOME HOME!

September 25, 2013.

POSTSCRIPT: As I was completing the supposedly last story of the book, I received a text from my daughter which made me smile. Another story had just taken shape - so here it is!

2013.
This is a true story.

"We can't afford that house, Mom. It's just out of reach." My daughter, now in her early forties, had been dreaming of a home on the bay for several years. Living for the last ten years in a large, rambling, shaker style two story home set on an acre lot near a lake, sounded perfect didn't it? So why would they now be considering another home? Well, they had purchased the shaker style for a bargain price. Being young and full of energy, the unkempt perennial gardens, rolling weed filled lawns, shallow well, low water pressure, soggy septic bed, aging hot tub, poor construction by an owner/ builder who was inexperienced, and wooden foundation were not insurmountable problems they had reasoned – the price was just so good for the size of the house and lot!

You don't have to be psychic to see what was coming next. The house became a veritable money pit!

But I am getting ahead of my story. This was their second house and I had had very little input. Not so with their first.

They had looked at a small home in town, one that suited a newly married couple's budget. In fact they had looked at everything for sale in town! When I arrived for a visit, they informed me they had seen a small two story home, but had decided against buying it for various reasons.

While out visiting other family in the area, I decided to take a look at it for myself. As I pulled up in front of it, I knew. This was to be their first home. I 'saw' them sitting on the front veranda – the very veranda where, a year later, I was informed I was to be a grandmother for the very first time!

Yes, they went back a second time, put in an offer and bought the house!

It turned out to be a good purchase. They lived happily there for a few years and then sold at a substantial profit. They were movin' on up!

That's when they bought the 'money pit!

I'm not saying they were unhappy there, but as another grandchild arrived, my daughter soon afterward returning to a full time teaching career, my son-in-law working full time and coaching hockey, and both very involved in the community, you can see how this 'high maintenance' house just did not live up to my daughter's dream! Warm and welcoming in spite of something always overflowing, leaking, breaking down or just not working, she still managed to make it feel like home.

Her father became her full time repair man which was symbolic, I thought, of the repair work done on their relationship, but that is not this story!

Ten years passed and she never gave up her dream of living in a spacious, new home where everything worked. Lately, a real estate agent had become her best friend, as she poured over every new listing. This went on for over two years. It was obvious to me that with such intensity of focus, the universe would simply have to align itself with her dream sooner or later!

You see, just as I do, she believes, 'what you think about, you bring about- your thoughts create your reality!'

So here I was visiting once again, when after an afternoon by the bay, she said,

"C'mon, Mom, I'll show you the houses we're looking at. We've narrowed it down to two. The one I really want has a trail leading to the bay and it's a beautiful new builder's home, but he just won't budge on the price and it's just out of our reach financially. We're most likely going to buy the other one."

At this point, the 'money pit, hadn't sold, but our visit to a psychic - yes, even psychics go to psychics - had told her, 'it will sell faster than you think.'

We jumped in our cars. I was planning to head home from there so I was driving my own vehicle. We pulled up in front of a lovely new house – the one she felt they would buy even though it was not located where she wanted to be, and I thought, "Hmm, nice, but not home."

Next we pulled into the cul-de-sac by the bay, and as I rounded the curve, I started to chuckle. Pulling up in front of this house, all I heard in my head was, "Welcome home!" This was it! This beautiful builder's home with the trail to her beloved bay was her new home! I knew it!

Already she was pulling away, heading home to a busy evening. We honked and waved goodbye and as I continued to drive, I was filled with joy that my daughter was about to manifest one of the biggest dreams of her life. Calling from my car - hands free of course, safety first! - I laughed as she answered, and I said, "Welcome home! That's your new house!"

Well, you know her answer. It is the opening statement of this story!

But, how does it all end, you wonder? Was my prediction right?

The 'money pit, sold a week later to a handy man and his family; some extra financing was approved along with a substantial gift from her father - her permanent repair man - and as I was writing the supposedly last story of this book, her text came through. -

"We got the house – you were right – again!"

Don't you just love happy endings?

I do!!

My end, but your beginning? Do you dare to turn the page and test your psychic ability?!

TIPS FOR DEVELOPING YOUR INTUITIVE (PSYCHIC) POWER

Let's start with a quiz to see where you are now. But before we begin, did you know?

According to Life magazine, **sixty per cent** of Americans believe they have had at least one psychic experience in their life.

Are you one of them? If so, it may be an indicator of psychic ability. Furthermore, if you are reading this you definitely have an interest in the subject and a desire to develop your intuitive abilities. I refer to psychic ability also as intuitive ability, for I have experienced they are the same, differing only in level of development. It is my belief that the creative force of the universe never gives a desire without the corresponding ability to bring about its manifestation. So let's begin!

About that psychic experience you may have had, you will soon see its significance!!

Let's start exploring your level of development by reflecting upon a few simple questions.

PSYCHIC ABILITY QUIZ

1. Is anyone in your family psychic? There seems to be a genetic component inherent in the ability. However, it can often skip generations as well. Don't just ask your parents, give grandma a call too.
2. Have you ever had a psychic experience? Perhaps you have seen an apparition, heard a voice when there was no one around, foreseen a future event or known what a friend was going to say or was feeling before they made it known.
3. Are you a highly anxious person? With scans scientist now can observe the brain wave patterns of psychics and have discovered the area engaged during a psychic reading is the area also responsible for producing feelings of anxiety! And you just thought you were a nervous Nellie!! No, you may be gifted psychically!
4. Do you just 'know' things without having to reason them through? Psychic insight comes as a gestalt or as whole thought. It seems to land in your brain complete without any inductive or deductive reasoning involved. It appears to come from 'somewhere else' and is accompanied by a deep feeling of accuracy!
5. Do you ever get 'goose bumps' when you say something to another person and it's as if you were thinking the same thing at the same time?
6. Have you ever had a feeling of pressure at the back of your neck when meditating? This can be an indication of messages from the intuitive self wanting to have expression through you.

HOW DID YOU DO? FOR COMPARISON I HAVE LISTED MY ANSWERS

1. I had a mother who could see auras and a maternal grandmother who could see apparitions.
2. I was first visited at age five by two spiritual beings.
3. I have always been a type 'A' personality and some would say I was driven.
4. With practice I have come to know the difference between information from the ego and information from the higher intuitive self. The higher self never argues. Clear and complete answers are given.
5. This very response is how I know I have, 'hit the nail on the head', during a reading!
6. The sensation of a pressure on the back of the neck indicating the desire to, 'speak intuitive truth', was acknowledged by another medium as she assisted me with my very first channeling. The experience and others describing my development as a psychic are documented in my novel, "The Sovereign Soul – A Story of Personal Power".

Keep in mind, this is by no means a definitive test of psychic ability or lack thereof. We are all unique and if you have the desire to develop your ability, then by my definition, you have the capability. However, I have always believed a desire, in order to manifest, must become a goal. What exactly do I mean by that? Well, a goal is a desire with a plan or what I like to call a, 'stratatude'!! What's a 'stratatude' you ask? It's a strategy with an attitude!

You see, if you don't have the right attitude, you most likely will not bother to have a strategy! Without a plan, you will spend your time reacting to life rather than creating the life you desire.

That's where your GPS comes in. Remember you have a Guided Personal Script—your intuitive self knows who you truly are, why you are here, and what makes you feel fulfilled! In other words, intuition guides you to follow the footsteps left by your destiny! When you lose the belief that your ego knows it all and trust enough to listen to your intuition, that's the right 'stratatude'! Sounds simple doesn't it? But there was a really big word in that last sentence—TRUST! It's the first step—believing in a power greater than your ego. The next step is to believe you are worthy of a wonderful life and the third is to connect with your intuitive power. How do you do this, you ask? By recognizing that what you accept as truth is simply a belief that has come into manifestation because of the energy given to it by you and/or by the collective consciousness. Change the belief; change the manifestation. Develop new 'stratatudes'!

A part of this change in belief is the willingness to forgive. Forgiveness of the self and others releases us from self destructive behaviour patterns and consequent suffering. Atonement is synonymous with forgiveness, but when the word is looked at more closely it can be seen as At-One-Ment. It is the alignment of the self with Divine creative energy through the processes of forgiveness— coming to understand and accept we are truly all one— and that to harm another is to harm the self and to forgive another is to forgive the self. The daily practice of love for yourself and others in all situations clears your frequency of negative interference, making you more open to divine guidance.

All stratatudes require action. Regular meditation is how to align yourself with your GPS. Divine guidance is always being broadcast, but if you aren't tuned into its frequency, you just won't get it no matter how hard you try! It's like setting your radio dial for news and expecting music! The receiver must be tuned into the sender! You must set the dial, turn on your receiver and make time to listen!

You know what I say—why would you trust what anyone tells you unless you have tested it? If you are willing to go for it, here are the 'stratatudes' I used to come to trust what I have just written to be Truth. Test them! Did they work for me you ask? You be the judge. I am in my sixties now and in perfect health, independently wealthy and happy. Humbly I would offer that I have achieved everything I have set out to do in this life, have no regrets, and my only desire is to be useful!

CASANDRA'S 'STRATATUDES'—STRATEGIES WITH ATTITUDE!

'Stratatudes to Access Your GPS!'

Your 'GPS' is your Guided Personal Script, or what some may call, your destiny! I believe you create your own life movie and as such also write its script. I also believe in 'rewrites'! That is, if you change your thoughts, you change your outcomes. Let's imagine there are unlimited possibilities of outcomes (scripts) and that through accessing your own intuition, you get to take action designed to produce the most desired outcome and or avoid undesired outcomes! Makes you think doesn't it? Recognize this truism?

> **Knowing what is happening around you is not nearly as important as what you think about what is happening around you.**

Stratatude: Set Clearly Defined, Time Sensitive Goals

1. Plan your work and work your plan—-this means that you actually have a plan (goals) and that you get off your butt and **do** something!
2. Set a time frame—without a definite date for achieving your plan it is simply a desire.

3. Write down your plan! This step helps your conscious mind get clear and let's your subconscious mind know you are serious. It will begin to look for opportunities that you might have missed otherwise.
4. Take action. Even small changes in behaviour can produce large changes in results over time.
5. Track your progress; revaluate if needed; celebrate your achievements.

Stratatude: Maintain a Healthy & Fit Physical Self

Physical Requirements for Psychic Power:

1. strong core muscles to channel energy –
2. good nutrition and hydration
3. healing of all physical imbalances – disease, chronic pain
4. freedom from all addictions

Let's look at each of these requirements in turn:

1. **strong core muscles**—my experience with back pain led to my discovery of yoga, swimming, walking, and weight lifting. Daily, varied exercise became my lifestyle.
2. **nutrition and hydration**—my research and discoveries led me to a regimen with included a diet rich in fruits, vegetables, nuts, fish, supplements, four to six glasses of water daily; reduced consumption of red meat, dairy, and sodium. Severely restricted items are: white sugar & white flour, wheat; and total removal of alcohol, artificial sweeteners (aspartame), and soda pop. I consume three small meals each day with an afternoon snack if desired and with no food after eight p.m. Food is fuel. It is not my friend. I do not intend to dig my grave with my teeth! Just a note here about alcohol—I have been a social drinker in

the past, but find now that consumption of 'spirits' lowers my vibration and limits my access to spirit!
3. **healing of the body**— incorporate traditional medicine, naturopathy, energy healing, reiki, nutrition, all healing modalities. Be your body's advocate – investigate. Talk to your body in meditation and ask what it requires in order to heal itself. Change what needs to be changed! Strive for balance and healthy habits. Be consistent and patient! Monitor all thoughts and check in with your emotions – your built in GPS! Louise Hay maintains that all illness is emotionally based and can be corrected through the appropriate affirmations.
4. **freedom from addictions**—what is an addiction? It is an attachment to a substance, behaviour, person—anything external to the self, which prevents intimacy with the self. It is in control, gains a position of uppermost importance to the individual, and is placed before anything else in the individual's life. Thus, a balanced, integrated and autonomous psyche becomes impossible. Addictions must first be acknowledged. Denial is a powerful tool which keeps the ego in charge and allows the continuation of the addictive behaviour—even beyond all reason—when the addiction has clearly become counter productive to a healthy lifestyle. The following are the most prevalent forms of addiction: alcoholism, workaholism, shopping, over eating, need for control, drama creation, rage, and victim hood. Twelve Step programs offer support and counseling facilitates honest self examination and this two pronged approach can often succeed in a release from bondage! It is a process, a journey back to sovereignty!

Stratatude: Develop the Mental Self

Development of both brain hemispheres:

Slow your mind. Modern life tends to wind us up; literally speeding up our brainwave frequency. Normal daily, wide-awake, states of consciousness are Beta frequency of fourteen up to twenty cycles per second. Beta level brainwave activity is too fast to allow psychic connections. Beta brain is a busy brain so the practice of meditation and relaxation methods is the **first step to develop psychic ability**. Also, have you ever wondered why children often have imaginary playmates? Up to the age of about seven years our brainwave frequency while awake is ALPHA. Alpha brainwave frequency is fourteen to seven cycles per second when measured on an EEG-an Electroencephalogram or brain wave test. Most of us loose these abilities past seven years of age as that is when our brainwave activity speeds up along with our intellect and thinking skills—we become 'socialized'. Luckily, with a little training and understanding, we can slow down our busy minds. **Calming down enough to access these states of mind is essential in developing psychic ability.** Some of us maintain our psychic gifts into adult life and can continue to drop back into Alpha and even Theta (seven to five cycles per second) states. Most of us do not know how it happens and may discover the ability accidentally, but in doing so we keep and further develop our psychic skills. **Like any skill, it gets better with practice.** The brain wave frequency of Alpha is the open channel to our subconscious, our imagination and creativity and to our sixth sense. With my research into the subject of psychic ability—and I highly recommend doing your own research as this book is simply an overview of a vast topic— I have learned that the Earth's heartbeat–known as the Schumann Resonance after the 1930s physicist Heinrich Schumann-discovered the permanent standing wave in the atmosphere resonates between the Earth's surface and the ionosphere predominantly at 7.8Hz. Thus, any artistic pursuits such as writing, drawing, painting, crafts, dancing and creating of beauty in all its forms aids in the development of psychic abilities. Also, **integration of the right brain**—creative and intuitive, gestalt knowing— **with the left brain**—logic, deductive and inductive reasoning— through meditation, use of non dominant side of body, cross wiring-using opposite sides of the body together- develop a relationship between the two modes of receiving and interpreting input – i.e. psychic ability or 'knowing' – head and heart knowledge! Slowing down will also save you time! Sounds like a paradox doesn't it? You will find that slowing your thoughts will allow for greater focus and concentration—being totally present within whatever activity you are engaged—thus making fewer mistakes and causing far less physical damage to yourself, property and others! It is also a great help in social interactions for it allows one to, 'think before speaking', resulting in far fewer apologies!

Acknowledgment of the ability:

Accept that psychic or intuitive abilities exist and that they are present within you to develop. Although this might sound silly or trite, **begin by telling yourself that you are psychic**. Make it a mantra that you repeat to yourself daily and often. This kind of self-talk has a scientific basis. It is now known that when a person learns something- whether it's a physical skill like wood carving or a mental exercise like memorizing poetry- through repetition, his or her brain physically changes—it "rewires" itself, if you will—to accommodate that task. This process of rewiring your brain for psychic ability begins with your belief in it.

1. **Read about the subject.** Knowledge will help, as you need some understanding of how things work. Adopt the policy you would take with a new hobby. Become involved in it, buy books and magazines, and look for more information on the Internet.
2. **Understand the Role of the EGO.** Understanding the role your conscious mind or 'ego' plays in blocking the development of your intuition is critical in developing your intuitive abilities. The mind is like a wonderful computer and its job is to meet challenges and solve problems; that is, to keep us safe and ensure our survival, but it hates to be out of work! It then logically follows that if the mind is in control of your life **at all**

times, you will have challenges and problems **at all times**! With nothing but challenges and problems manifesting in your daily life, you will be in a reactive state rather than charting your own course. Thus, when there is no apparent danger—which is most of the time in our modern lives—a technique I often use when the ego brings forth the following-worst case scenario, reasons why something I want won't happen, fear, self-deprecating or negative thoughts-I simply thank it for sharing and change the focus to something pleasant or desirable. Thankfully, the ego can be distracted, refocused and reprogrammed to be used in service of the intuitive higher self! It is a useful and accurate computer, but should never be writing the programme!

3. **Encourage your insights and speak your truth.** When you have an intuitive 'knowing' about something, record it or share it with someone you trust. Keep a written record of your insights and predictions to check for accuracy. In my experience, when I found the courage to speak my predictions, they increased in frequency and accuracy. It's as if it, 'primes the pump'!

4. **Keep a journal.** Journal writing helps get in touch with your thoughts and feelings and helps 'clear the decks' of internal negative chatter and unnecessary emotional drama.

5. **Record your dreams and learn about dream symbolism.** There are many good books to help with this. Some dreams can be prophetic (they are usually much more emotionally charged than regular dreams). Pay attention to a dream which invokes great emotion and lingers in memory.

6. **Practise automatic writing which is writing with the non dominant hand while in a meditative state.** This can be a very insightful technique and is often useful in removing mental blocks with regard to emotional issues. (There are also books written on this technique)

7. **Practise SCANNING with a partner.** While both in a meditative state, face a partner and 'scan' them for insights. Share without censoring the information received. You will

often be amazed at what you can learn about even a total stranger! (Note: This will only work if you have the consent of the person being scanned. We all have 'protective shields' when it comes to revealing information to a psychic probe!)

8. **Make predictions—record and date them!** Check back later for accuracy. When a few come to pass that will encourage you and when more than 50% come true (better than the odds), you're on your way!!!

9. **Learn to meditate**. Meditation is the most important task to mastering the quieting of the mind so that psychic messages may be received. **Practice daily meditation.**—15 to 20 minutes or more every day is ideal, but you can start with a little as 5 minutes and build it consistently. This will strengthen the ability to tune into the intuitive higher self and access your GPS! (see meditation methods which follow)

MEDITATION: DEFINITION AND METHODS

Definition:

Meditation is the process of narrowing the focus of the mind through continuous and contemplative thought. The mind has a natural propensity for motion. To will the mind to be still only compounds the problem. The mind will begin to settle in stillness, however, if given something to focus upon. This helps draw the conscious mind inward. There are three major ways of engaging this process.

Methods:

I. Use a mantra—a sacred word or statement of truth or object such as a burning candle— as the focus of awareness. This functions like an anchor on a ship which is trying to remain still on a stormy sea. If the mind drifts in waves of thinking, bring awareness back to the anchor, the mantra. Focus on a single word, statement of truth, or object will often result in revelation, or may take you to a deeper level of silence.

II. Watch thoughts without attachment. Become the observer or the witness. If a person is stared at for an extended period of time, he or she will look away. Thoughts respond in very much the same way. If we stare at them without emotional attachment, they will soon turn away and drift into the ocean of consciousness.

III. Guided meditation through the use of CD's as well as classes where meditation is led by others. This may be an excellent way to begin conditioning your mind. It's similar to using 'training wheels' when you first learned to ride your bike!

STRATATUDE: LEARN TO DETACH FROM THE EMOTIONAL SELF

Recognize this? "Suffering is only necessary until you realize it is unnecessary." Eckhart Tolle
"Suffering is optional." Byron Katie

EMOTIONAL DETACHMENT AND THE POWER OF THE EGO

I believe that as young children we are aware of our divine connection—we are psychic! How is that we lose that ability? Don Miguel Ruiz in his book, "The Four Agreements" refers to the process as the 'domestication of humans' In my novel, "The Sovereign Soul", I chronicle the socialization of the main character, Lexie, as she is conditioned by society to relinquish her power a little at a time and come to believe in the collective dream. What is that dream and how is it we are drawn in?

We are put to 'sleep' by being taught the following: to trust others' opinions and beliefs more than our own feelings; to refrain from speaking our truth and expressing our feelings; to make assumptions rather than seeking clarification often feeling misunderstood as a consequence; to judge everyone and everything we experience as either good or bad rather than neutral, often in order to feel superior; and to trust our intellect and **fear our emotions**. We fear our emotions because we have been socialized to believe we have no control over them. This socialization effectively cuts us off from our intuitive self and the creative source thus denying our connection to all that is, establishing instead the perception of ourselves as separate and alone. Is it any wonder we are left wondering why we feel lost?

The solution is to recognize that you are more than your mind or your feelings. You can choose what the mind believes and what it will focus upon and thus control your feelings and what you manifest in your reality! WOW!! What knowledge! Is it any wonder why so many egos in our world do not wish this knowledge to be main stream? Knowledge is indeed power. Your mind is a tool for you to use just as you use a computer or any other aid to perception. To know and apply this is a 'stratatude' that will lead you to be proactive and in charge of your own life!

A Test for Truth:

If you want to demonstrate how your thoughts and their resulting emotions are empowering or disempowering try this test for truth using the technique of 'arm testing' with a partner.

Stand facing one another. Raise your extended arms to shoulder height and think a positive thought that evokes a good feeling. Have your partner place his or her hand on your wrist and exert downward pressure. Note the strength of your resistance. Now think a negative thought that evokes a bad feeling—this shouldn't be too difficult as we all tend to beat ourselves up in our self talk—and have your partner exert the same downward pressure on your wrist. Note your strength of resistance.

Surprised by the result? Negative thoughts and their resulting emotions (fear, anger, depression, guilt, envy to name a few) weaken us! How many times a day do you weaken yourself?

Remember: Thoughts held in mind produce after their kind. What you think about, you bring about. You create your own reality through your perceptions and interpretations! Yep, you write your own movie script!

Remember this? There are no victims, only volunteers. This is one of the hardest beliefs to accept because we all want to blame someone else for our troubles. You can continue to do that for as long as you like. You have free will; however, nothing changes if nothing changes. Change you attitude, adopt some new strategies and change your life. Keep reading— not just this book but the dozens of books that will help you get clear on this 'stratatude'.

Your emotions are one way your intuitive self speaks to you. We ignore them at our peril for if suppressed they can make us physically ill. Learning how to deal with them in a positive and constructive way is one of the biggest challenges we face in life. Until the emotional chatter is cleared

from the mind, very little intuitive guidance can be heard. There are many ways to clear old emotional issues—counseling, twelve step programmes, journal writing, meditation, rigorous honesty, making amends, coming out of denial and taking responsibility for our own actions, forgiveness work— these are some of the more powerful ways to become emotionally healthy and psychically open.

Here's a 'stratatude' I use often to deal with emotions:

Check in with your emotional state regularly and– **name it, claim it, and tame it!**

We often don't even know what we are feeling so identifying the feeling and giving it a name (sadness, anger, jealousy, joy to name but a few) helps us to get clear about what we are feeling. As children many of us were not questioned nor listened to about what we were feeling and consequently did not learn to name our emotions. Parents often felt threatened by our feelings—they had not been taught how to express them either—so they would often 'shut us down' or distract us to avoid feeling uncomfortable themselves.

Claiming your feelings refers to accepting the fact that is normal and acceptable to feel as you do even if others tell you otherwise. It is disrespectful to tell another individual that they should not feel as they do. Feelings are neither right nor wrong; they just are.

Taming your feelings means that you deal with your emotions in socially acceptable ways. You don't become a human volcano erupting with anger every time you feel like it nor do you inflict your bad moods upon others. I have been known to take a baseball bat to a cushion or yell while driving alone in the car. It may get you some pretty strange looks, but at least no one gets hurt and I feel better.

Is attaining emotional health easy? No. I once had a friend—a big, strapping firefighter tell me— "I can carry people out of burning buildings, but I can't tell my buddy he has a drinking problem."

I do understand that many of the Truisms in this book may, 'rattle your cage', but that may be a good thing. I do not ask that you accept my Truths, but only that you be open to the possibility of acceptance.

That leads me to the next area of development.

STRATATUDE: DEVELOP THE SPIRITUAL SELF

Truism: "Coincidence is God's way of remaining anonymous. There is only one question to ask. Is this a friendly universe?" Albert Einstein

I believe I am a spiritual being having a physical experience and I believe old Albert answered his question with a 'yes'!

What are your spiritual beliefs? Please recognize that they are simply beliefs, not truths. Do they empower you? Or do they fill you with guilt? You can change your beliefs and thus change your outcomes.

Casandra's Concept of Practical Spirituality

I like things that work. Ideas and concepts are wonderful, but so often they feel like mental masturbation—they make us feel good, but accomplish nothing! Did I mention that I am a type 'A' personality? That means I like results! I would not be writing the tips and truisms part of this book if I had not tested them for truth and found that they do indeed work! Don't take my word for it—try them for yourself. You can blindly believe what you have been taught, buying into the collective dream (or nightmare?), or you can wake up and connect with your inner wisdom and become a fully self actualized person. To awaken takes rigorous self examination and honesty. Courage is needed to have integrity of the word; that is, to say what you mean and mean what you say; but it will develop congruency between head and heart and lead to inner peace. Self-actualized beings share these characteristics: self confidence in their own insights—they give no power to what others think of them; they don't take anything personally; they make no assumptions, investigating to find the facts for themselves; they have no attachment to outcomes thus no manipulation of people or events; and they make no judgments only evaluations—in other words, they do not engage in gossiping.

Develop a daily spiritual practice:

- yoga for breathing and strengthening of the core muscles, nutritious diet and hydration for physical balancing.
- thought monitoring for intellectual balancing
- journal writing (rigorous self-examination) and dream interpretation for emotional balancing
- daily meditation—10 or more minutes each day to achieve spiritual balancing and connect with your GPS – Great Personal Source
- integrity of the word—say what you mean and mean what you say—for relationship balancing

A disciplined spiritual practice leads to wisdom. 'Awake and aware' enlightened human beings with a heightened sense of the divine nature of being know that to be is enough—their higher vibration alone is of value to this planet. You become a human being instead of a human doing! At the higher vibration of love you can change or influence people and events just by being present and you can become 'seers' able to discern future events!

STRATATUDE: DEVELOP THE RELATIONSHIP WITH SELF

Perhaps I have left the topic of relationships to the end for it seems to be the area of greatest challenge in my life. Married now for the third time—the third time's the charm they say—I really relate to the women who lament, "Where are all the good men?"

It took me almost sixty years to realize that I wasn't about to attract a 'good' man until I became a 'good' woman! Like attracts like! That's just not fair, you say! Well, remember, every time we argue with reality, we lose.

Face it. We are often so busy looking for the perfect partner to build our lives around; we forget that our lives should be built around ourselves. Yes, I heard the collective gasp, especially from you ladies— the ones who were taught that to put yourself first was— dare I say it—SELFISH!

We need to bake our own cake! The partner is the frosting!

So it looks like you've first got to become what you're looking for! Most of the women in my workshops when asked to make a list of the qualities they want in a man will write something like the following:

- Rich
- Handsome
- Rich
- Honest
- Rich
- Dependable
- Rich
- Loyal
- Rich
- Good communicator

See a theme here? When I look over their lists, I make just one comment. "Are you those things?"

- Are **you** financially stable and responsible; never mind rich? Or are you waiting for 'prince charming' to rescue you and pay off your debts?
- Are **you** attractive and fit? Have you lost that weight yet? (Men are visual creatures. If they don't like what they see on the outside, the odds are good they won't get to know what's on the inside. Shallow, aren't they? Maybe so, but you know what I say about arguing with reality!)
- Are **you** dependable? Do you follow up on what you have committed to do?
- Are **you** willing to commit or do **you** keep looking for something better to come along?
- Are **you** good at communicating what you want and need? Do **you** say what you mean and mean what you say?

Like attracts like—if you want to know what kind of person you are, look at your relationships! Those who show up in our lives are our greatest teachers because they mirror our best and worst qualities!

In conclusion, here is what I have learned from the men in my life: You don't have to be psychic to get this, but it does help to listen to your intuition in this area! Deep down we really do know the truth.

- Men and women are different. We all know this, right? Then why is it that you ladies treat men as if they were a girlfriend and you men think your ladies like what your buddies like?
- Men and women's brains are wired differently and we want different things. Women put relationships first but most men don't. Brutal but true.
- Men like the challenge of pursuing a woman. If a woman is too 'easy' men will lose interest.

- Nagging doesn't work. If you're nagging you're still available to him. Try saying what you want and leaving the room, house, or city (even better) for a few hours or days. That is the best way to get his attention!
- Self confidence is sexy. If a man/woman doesn't want a confident, self-actualized woman/man, you don't want him/her.
- Abuse is never okay! It is never your fault if someone else loses control and abuses you. It is their issue!
- You do train people how to treat you. Set up consequences for bad behaviour and follow through–always!
- Ask for what you want and need. No hinting—be clear and direct. Your partner is not a mind reader.
- Treat your partner the way you want to be treated!

I guess that last one pretty much sums up relationship 'stratatudes'!

One last thought on relationships for the ladies reading my book.

Men may be able to build their world, but they often like a woman to decorate it!

Well, this psychic is pretty much done telling her story, but I am going to end with some final tips and truisms—I like to have the last word. I call them:

CASANDRA'S FOURTEEN DAYS & WAYS TO FABULOUS–

(Adapted from, "The Four Spiritual Laws of Prosperity" by Edwene Gaines)

**A two week commitment to yourself -
Add a new task each day as you continue to practise all the others.**

Today I:

1. strive for order–the mystics call order heaven's first law–clean out the clutter in my home and work space, balance my cheque book and give away objects no longer needed
2. take time for solitude–I give myself the gift of being alone in the silence everyday
3. create beauty in my work space and my home as well as in my personal appearance
4. give myself a healthy treat–the universe will treat me only as well as I treat myself
5. tell the truth–the whole truth–I say what I mean and mean what I say- if I have lied to someone, I fix it
6. laugh–I celebrate my divine nature by finding humour in life–I watch a funny movie, enjoy a joke
7. remain calm– Divine Spirit is my source–always. When things are difficult I use the affirmation, 'All is well. Divine Spirit provides.'

8. appreciate others and tell them–I give genuine and public compliments
9. open my heart– I ask myself, 'what am I avoiding in my own life by not forgiving this person or situation?'
10. feed my spirit– I read, listen to a CD, pray or meditate –I make it a habit to turn within each day.
11. welcome change–I ask myself, 'what new opportunity will this change create?'
12. let go of all things that do not empower me or enrich my life. I take a thorough and honest inventory of my life.
13. do something new– I learn a new skill or expand my knowledge
14. express my gratitude –I find something to be grateful for.

At the end of the 14 day challenge, you will have incorporated these new practices into your life. Fasten your seat belt – you're about to fly! You will be FABULOUS!

LOVE & BLESSINGS
CASANDRA!

ARE YOU PSYCHIC? WOULD YOU LIKE TO BE PUBLISHED?

According to Life magazine over sixty per cent of us have had psychic experiences. I believe it is even higher than that.

PUBLISH YOUR STORY WITH US!

Help us to spread the word that we are all gifted with intuitive insight and that we all have a built in 'GPS'!

We would be happy to receive and review your story submission and, if accepted, publish it in future volumes of, ***Adventures of Mystic Mediums – Amazing True Psychic Stories***. Receipt of submission constitutes permission for publication.

Send your submission to **mymysticmedium@gmail.com**

I understand many of us have a 'book in us' but, regretfully we cannot accept unsolicited manuscripts.

Enjoy reading more amazing stories on the website **www.amazingmysticmedium.com**

PERSONAL READINGS by CASANDRA:

Casandra has done hundreds of psychic readings for clients all across North America either in person or over the telephone. If you would like a personal psychic reading send your request to **mymysticmedium@gmail.com** and you will be contacted to set up your appointment.

Love & blessings to all my fellow mystics!
Casandra

ABOUT THE AUTHOR

Casandra Hart, a retired teacher and business owner, is much in demand as a psychic and medium, author, speaker, spiritual counselor and ordained non-denominational minister.

Happily residing for six months in beautiful Ontario cottage country, she spends the winter months in equally beautiful Naples, Florida. She can be contacted for private readings at **mymysticmedium@gmail.com**.

BIBLIOGRAPHY

1. Andy Rooney, *Andy Rooney Praises Women Over Fifty*, www.drbj.hubpages.com /2013.
2. Byron Katie with Stephen Mitchell, *Loving What Is*, (Harmony Books, 2002).
3. Carl Yung, www.goodreads.com, /2013.
4. Catherine Aird, *His Burial Too*, www.catherineaird.com/2013.
5. Eckhart Tolle, www.spiritual-experiences.com , /2013.
6. Gary Renard, *The Disappearance of the Universe*, (Fearless Books 2003).
7. George Saunders, *Graduation Speech*, www.huffingtonpost.com /2013/08/01.
8. Helen Schucman, *The Course in Miracles*, (Foundation for Inner Peace, 1976).
9. Kahil Gibran, *The Prophet*, (Alfred A.Knopf 1923).
10. Louise Hay, www.goal-setting-motivation.com /inspirational-quotes-by-women/ 2013.
11. Margaret Thatcher, www.goodreads.com /589553/ 2013.
12. Socrates, www.goodreads.com,/ 2013.
13. Wayne Dyer, www.brainyquote.com /2013.

CPSIA information can be obtained at www.ICGtesting.com
Printed in the USA
LVOW06s0552240414

382956LV00001B/22/P